Affordable Landscaping

Created and designed by
the editorial staff of
ORTHO BOOKS

Editor
Sally W. Smith

Writer
Michael D. Smith

Designer
Gary Hespenheide

Ortho Books

Publisher
Robert B. Loperena

Editorial Director
Christine Jordan

Manufacturing Director
Ernie S. Tasaki

Managing Editors
Robert J. Beckstrom
Michael D. Smith
Sally W. Smith

Prepress Supervisor
Linda M. Bouchard

Editorial Assistants
Joni Christiansen
Sally J. French

Address all inquiries to
Ortho Books
Box 5006
San Ramon, CA 94583-0906

Copyright © 1995
Monsanto Company
All rights reserved under international and Pan-American copyright conventions.

1 2 3 4 5 6 7 8 9
95 96 97 98 99 2000

ISBN 0-89721-274-6
Library of Congress Catalog Card Number 94-67708

THE SOLARIS GROUP
2527 Camino Ramon
San Ramon, CA 94583-0906

Acknowledgments

Editorial Coordinator
Cass Dempsey

Copyeditor
Toni Murray

Proofreader
Alicia K. Eckley

Indexer
Trisha Lamb Feuerstein

Illustrators
Deborah Cowder, Indigo Design & Imaging
Mitzi McCarthy
Robyn Sherrill Menigoz

Separations by
Color Tech. Corp.

Lithographed in the U.S.A. by
Banta Company

Consultants
Roger Fiske, Fiske Landscaping, San Ramon, Calif.
Gary Thornton, Thornton Gardens, Maineville, Ohio

Designers
Names of designers are followed by the page numbers on which their work appears.
R = right, C = center, L = left, T = top, B = bottom.

Janan Apaydin, Apaydin Ecoscapes, Oakland, Calif.: 8T
Michele Schaal, San Francisco, Calif.: 37T, 43
Roger Peters: 39

Special Thanks to:
California Redwood Association
Auguste Broucaret
City College of San Francisco
Deborah Cowder
Buz and Terry Derenink
Peggy Henry
Shari Marks and Troy Wiggins
Therese O'Connor and Keith Shandalow
Jana Olsen
Susan Pieper
R & D Concrete Contracting, Santa Rosa, Calif.
Robert Rakka Construction, Sonoma, Calif.
Pat Sajor
Shamrock Building Materials, Santa Rosa, Calif.
Wedekind's Garden Center, Sonoma, Calif.

Photographers
Names of photographers are followed by the page numbers on which their work appears.
R = right, C = center, L = left, T = top, B = bottom.

Laurie A. Black: 6B, 28B
Richard Christman: 56
Josephine Coatsworth: 28T, 34T
Alan Copeland: 35, 48, 71, 76, 88
Mary Ann Evans: 8B
Barbara J. Ferguson: 40
David Goldberg: 7T, 8T, 12, 37T, 43, 54, 55, 59, 91
Saxon Holt: Front and back covers, 4–5, 7BR, 10–11, 14, 19, 20–21, 29B, 34B, 37B, 52–53, 57, 58T, 58B, 69T, 69B, 70, 77, 80–81, 83, 91
Balthazar Korab: 39
Michael Landis: 9, 22, 31T
Michael McKinley: 1, 7BL, 30
James K. McNair: 31B, 32
Leslie M. Newman: 29T
Kenneth Rice: 38
Richard Shiell: 41
Tom Tracy: 6T
Doreen L. Wynja: 36, 42

Front Cover
Top left: A careful investigation of your site helps you plan the garden that will best meet your family's needs.
Top right: Ground limestone marks lines for irrigation ditches.
Bottom left: If field or river stones are available for free, they provide an inexpensive way to bring an elegant touch to the landscape.
Bottom right: When your landscaping progresses to the point of planting flower beds, you're almost done!

Title Page
Providing bright color for the entire summer, an annual bed can be started economically with seeds and small plants.

Back Cover
A newly installed landscape with small plants looks sparse at first, but as the plants grow, they fill the space and bring the plan to life.

The Inexpensive Landscape

Go ahead and dream—landscaping <u>can</u> be done on a shoestring. Even with a limited budget, you can have a yard to be proud of.

Gardens are inherently low-cost. For eons, people have made beautiful gardens with slips from the neighbor's plants, seeds collected from the meadow, and manure from the barn. These methods still work, and versions of them are described in this book. For instance, for a few dollars, you can buy enough seed to plant hundreds of square feet of garden. You can root cuttings from your neighbor's hedge to make a hedge of your own.

If your interests and time don't allow you to start your own plants, however, you can still landscape your yard within a limited budget. Some features and materials are much less expensive than others. This book tells you about them and offers dozens of money-saving tips for the home landscaper. It assumes you want results fairly quickly, but that you don't have enough money to build the garden of your dreams . . . at least, not all at once. It proposes that you create a starter landscape that provides a solid foundation on which to build as your finances permit. You will have all the essentials, and your yard will look attractive and fill your family's needs—but the swimming pool, spa, and outdoor cooking station can wait for a few years. This type of landscaping is like starting with a simple one-bedroom house, then adding rooms as your family grows.

The book also assumes that you are doing a complete landscape, rather than just sprucing up the yard. Perhaps you are beginning with a new home surrounded by potential—and not much else. Or perhaps you have purchased an older home with a yard that has been neglected and needs to be rebuilt. In either case, you can install a finished landscape on a shoestring.

A low-cost landscape can be beautiful. Plan carefully, shop wisely—and invest time rather than money.

WHERE CAN YOU SAVE MONEY?

Most of your savings will come as a result of the decisions you make as you do your planning. This book guides you through these decisions, pointing out options for saving money and helping you select landscape features that won't break your budget.

Which Landscaping Elements Are Expensive?

The most expensive components of home landscapes are structures. Gazebos, decks, fences, walls, sheds, and barbecues cost hundreds or thousands of dollars. That doesn't mean you should ban structures, but you shouldn't plan to have too many. Those you do include should be small and simple. Luckily, structures are easy to add to a landscape later, when you can better afford them. For example, a spot overlooking a lovely view might just cry for a Victorian gazebo. For now, you can put a gravel sitting area there, with a couple of chairs and a table. Later, you will build a gazebo on the gravel and move the furniture into it.

The choice of building materials also influences the cost of a landscape. For instance, a slate patio, although beautiful, costs 10 times as much as a crushed limestone patio—which has its own appeal.

Although slate paths (top) and gazebos (bottom) are elegant garden features, they add greatly to the cost of landscaping. Include such graceful additions in your plans, but don't put them in yet. For now, live with concrete stepping-stones and a simple sitting area. Later, when you can afford it, add the more expensive elements.

The kinds of plants you select have less influence on the total cost of the landscape than their size does. The larger a plant is, the longer a nursery has had to care for it, and the more the nursery charges for it. Similarly, you can save hundreds of dollars just by planting a lawn from seed instead of laying sod.

The single easiest place to save money on your landscaping project is on the labor. This book assumes you will be doing most of the work yourself. Doing the work yourself not only saves you the cost of other people's time and expertise; it also gives you much more control over methods and materials, allowing you to save money on those, too. Most landscape contractors have methods of working that get a job done well and efficiently, but not always inexpensively. If you are willing to spend some time exploring for bargains and raising plants yourself—tasks a contractor is not likely to be willing to do—you can save considerable money. However, consider hiring help for heavy physical labor. A sturdy student will be a welcome and, in most cases, inexpensive assistant when you are digging ditches or clearing brush.

Lastly, the style you select influences the ultimate cost of the landscape. Formal gardens, usually rich in structures and expensive appointments, cost more to build than informal gardens, just as formal interior decor is usually

Crushed stone is an inexpensive alternative to slate. It provides a sitting area that blends in with this natural landscape (top), and a mulch that accents the house (bottom left) at a low cost.
Bottom right: Several years old, this large crape myrtle costs $275. A young plant in a 1-gallon container would cost about $5.

An attractive informal patio can be made of broken concrete slabs and homemade cast-concrete stepping-stones, with creeping thyme filling the spaces between the stones.

A spare and inexpensive landscape such as this one can serve for a few years, then be replaced by a more complex planting.

more expensive than informal. Traditional formal garden style includes stone or teak benches, fountains, and other expensive details. It also requires expensive materials and methods. For example, an informal path might be simply composed of rolled aggregate or a row of flat stones. A formal path is usually edged and is made of brick, tile, or some other hard paving material. In general, the more your garden looks like natural scenery, the less it will cost.

Working Within a Budget

Budgeting a landscaping job is no different from budgeting any other home improvement job. If the money available isn't enough to do everything right now, you will have to decide what to do now and what to leave for later. You have three options for building any landscape feature. You can do it just the way you want (the most expensive option), you can install a temporary version with the intention of upgrading it later, or you can delay building and do nothing about it now.

The first few steps of your landscaping project should be done well. You should do a thorough job of cleaning up your site. Then do the

The larger the tree, the greater its value as a landscape plant, so put in trees as early as possible. With time, they will dominate and enhance the yard as this one does.

grading and soil work without skimping. This is the foundation of your landscape. It is difficult to do this work once the landscape is installed, and it's important that it be done right to avoid problems such as flooding or erosion. Even though this work isn't very exciting, plan to make a good job of it.

Since patios and paths are easy to upgrade later, they are good candidates for temporary solutions. If you can't afford the patio you want, put in an inexpensive one for now; that will give you a place to eat breakfast outside on fine mornings or relax after dinner. An inexpensive patio can also substitute temporarily for a deck.

Plant the major trees and shrubs as early as possible. Trees take many years to mature and provide the benefits you want from them, so it's important to get them growing as soon as you can. Perennials, which mature in two or three years, and annuals, which mature in a single growing season, can be left for later.

The methods shown in this book will allow you to trade your time for money. You trade your time in two senses: You spend time doing the work instead of hiring somebody else to do it, and you invest time waiting until you can afford the more expensive items in your landscape. The more time you are able to put into making a low-cost landscape, the lower its cost will be in dollars. And the more items you can defer until a later date, the lower the cost of today's landscape. By making these tradeoffs, you can have a landscape that pleases you, makes you proud of your home, and allows you to extend your living area from the house into the yard . . . and you can have it now.

The Starting Point: Your Site

Begin your new landscape by assessing what you have. Then start mapping the possibilities.

The first task in planning a landscape is to study what you have. This chapter will tell you how to make a finished plan, drawn to scale, of the yard as it looks before you begin landscaping. This is called a *base map*. It will show the location of the house, property lines, and any features you decide to keep: paths, driveways, trees, shrubs. To the base map you will add information in graphic form—a tracing-paper overlay with notes about prevailing wind, sun exposure, good views and bad views, privacy problems, and erosion and drainage. The base map and notes are the beginning of your new landscape.

As you draw the base map, you will become intimately familiar with your yard. You will discover things about it you never knew, or rediscover things you had forgotten. You will sharpen your perceptions. For example, you will become aware that you have always disliked looking at your neighbor's garage door from your breakfast table or that the first rays of sun touching the top of the hill behind your garden fill you with joy.

The first step of planning is to study the existing situation. After mapping your site, make notes of the features you want to emphasize or minimize.

KNOW YOUR LIMITS

Even when you own your land, your rights to build on it are restricted. Before you begin planning, identify those restrictions. First, find out exactly where your property lines are. The apparent property lines—a hedge, fence line, or the edge of a lawn—are very often not the legal property lines. To be sure of the location

Begin mapping your site by trying to locate surveyor's markers at the corners. This iron bar, topped with a yellow cap for visibility, identifies a corner.

of your property lines, you must have the site surveyed. If you are willing to take a chance or if you don't plan to build an expensive structure near the property lines, you can locate them yourself.

You may already have a *plot plan*—a plan that shows the location of your property lines—as part of your deed. If not, get a copy of the plan from the tax assessor's office or building department. Surveyors often leave markers on the corners of the property. Try to find these markers to accurately locate the property lines. A marker may be a line scribed in the curb in front of your house or an iron pipe driven into the ground. The pipe may be covered with dirt—dig around a bit where you expect it to be. If you have trouble, ask your neighbors; they may know where the corner markers are. Once you find the first corner, use the distances shown on the plot plan to locate the other corners.

Within your property lines, you may have restrictions. In addition to property lines, the plot plan shows easements. An *easement* is someone else's right of access to a section of your property. The other party is usually an agency, such as a fire department or utility company, but sometimes it is another individual. An easement restricts you from placing

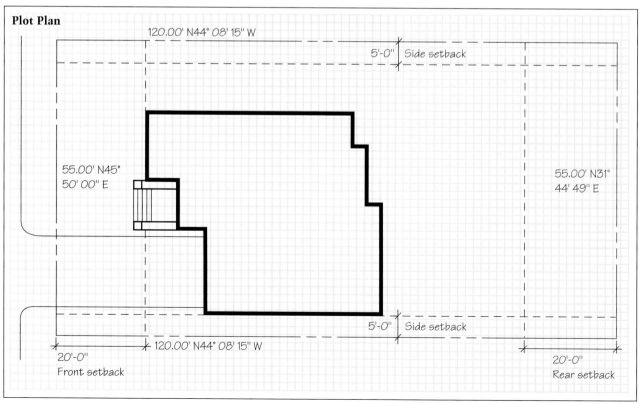

Plot Plan

120.00' N44° 08' 15" W

5'-0" | Side setback

55.00' N45° 50' 00" E

55.00' N31° 44' 49" E

5'-0" | Side setback

20'-0"
Front setback

120.00' N44° 08' 15" W

20'-0"
Rear setback

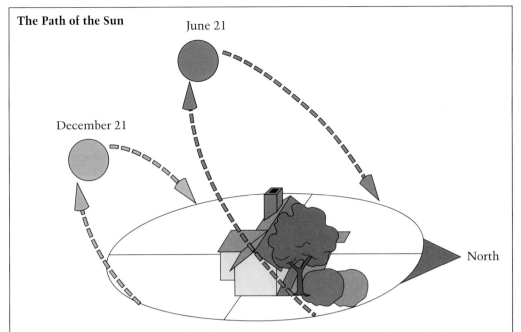

The Path of the Sun

June 21

December 21

North

The winter sun is lower in the sky than the summer sun, so it casts longer shadows. Think about where shadows will fall in summer and winter as well as at different times of day.

any structures, trees, or large shrubs that would block the other party's access.

Building departments often place limits on how close to the street and how close to adjacent properties you may build. The minimum distance you must allow is called a *setback*. Setbacks may not be shown on your plot plan; if not, ask the building department.

Homeowners' associations often impose building restrictions. Check your association agreement to determine what you can and can't do on your property.

MEASURING THE SITE

After locating your property lines and learning about building restrictions, the next step is to identify the positions of the buildings, trees, and paths on your site by measuring them and making notes on a map. Later, you will use these measurements to draw a base map.

You can save some work by taking notes on a copy of the plot plan. If the plan is small—as they often are—make an enlarged copy of it. If you don't have a plot plan, make a quick sketch of the major features of the property.

Getting Oriented

Begin the measuring process by locating true north. The simplest way is to find the North Star. If you don't know how to identify it, use a

compass to locate magnetic north (which is in the region of Hudson Bay, not at the North Pole) instead. If you are east of the Mississippi River, true north is very close to compass north. West of the Mississippi, true north is west of magnetic north, by a few degrees near the river, about 15 to 20 degrees on the Pacific Coast. Don't worry if you can't precisely locate true north. Just indicate it on your plan as accurately as possible. This will allow you to make note of where the sun travels across the sky and thus take account of where shadows fall as you design your landscape.

Plotting Major Features

Use a 50- or 100-foot tape measure to measure distances. If you have an assistant, one of you will hold each end of the tape. If you are working by yourself, secure the far end of the tape by poking a long screwdriver through the loop at the end and into the ground.

First, measure the house. Begin at one corner and lay the tape along one wall. On your map, label the beginning point of the tape with a letter, such as A. You will record measurements as distances from point A. Walking along the tape, record the distance to corners, windows, doors, and anything else you will need to be able to locate later. When you have recorded all the points along the tape, pick it up and

Measure significant dimensions of your property. Along each house wall, record the distance to any major element, such as where the fence meets this one.

Measuring Along a Line

To measure things in a straight line, such as the features on the side of a house, lay a tape along the line and record distances from the starting point, point A

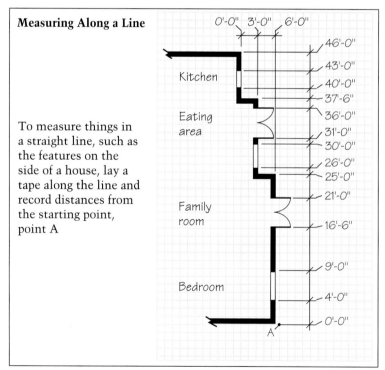

measure distances of objects from the tape line. For instance, if the wall has a bumpout or bay, you will have noted its two corners in the first measurement. Now measure the distance the wall sticks out. Measure the remaining walls of the house in the same way.

Next, determine the location of the property lines in relation to the house. If the lines are parallel to the house, measure the distance to each one from the nearest house wall. Measure that distance at two different places just to find out if the lines are truly parallel.

If the property lines are not parallel to the house walls, you will indicate the property corners on the map by triangulation. *Triangulation* uses measurements from two known points to locate a third, unknown one. In this case, the two known points are corners of your house. The unknown point is the property corner. Begin in your yard, by measuring the distance from one corner of the house to the property corner marker. Make a note of the measurement. Then measure the distance to the same marker from another corner of the house. Record this measurement. Later, when you draw your base map, you will be able to indicate the property corner using these two measurements. Take and record the measurements necessary to plot the remaining corners.

Now, in your yard, locate every other feature you think you might keep in the final landscape: trees, paths, shrubs, sheds, and other structures. If possible, measure the distance between the house wall and each feature. Approximate the position of the feature on the plot plan or sketch, mark it, and record the measurement. To plot the positions of isolated features, such as trees, use triangulation. Take the necessary measurements and record them on the plan. Measure items that are arranged in a line, such as a row of trees, in the same way you measured the house wall, by laying the tape down along the line and recording distances from the end point of the tape. Record the measurements.

Measuring Slope

If your site is flat or nearly so, or if it has a fairly consistent slope, it will probably not be necessary to measure the slope. But if the ground is uneven, and especially if you think it will need correcting, you'll have to map the slope. On the base map, you will use contour lines to represent the slope. A *contour line* is a line on a map that connects all the points on the ground that are at the same elevation. Begin slope mapping by selecting a contour interval, the vertical distance between contour lines. A convenient interval is 5 feet, but if the site is too steep or too flat for a 5-foot interval to be useful, select the interval that will work best for your purposes.

A simple way to measure slope is with a line level. This is a small spirit level that has two hooks so it can hang from a tightly stretched horizontal string. By keeping the bubble within marks on the device, you can keep the string perfectly level. To measure slope you will also need a length of strong string, a bundle of surveyor's stakes, a heavy hammer, and a large screwdriver with a blade at least 12 inches long.

Begin by tying a loop in the end of the string, putting the screwdriver through it, and poking the screwdriver into the ground on the highest point of the property. Hang the level on the string and, using the level to keep the string horizontal, and gradually raising your hand, walk downhill until the end of the string in your hand is 5 feet above the ground (or at whatever contour interval you have selected). An easy way to measure this height is to select a place on your body that is 5 feet above the ground. If this part is your chin, for instance, walk downhill until the level string is chin-high. Drive a stake into the ground at this point.

Now walk sideways along the slope, staying at the 5-foot level. Drive stakes as close as you feel necessary for accuracy. The rougher the ground, the closer the stakes should be.

Once you have marked the 5-foot contour, move the end of the string to a location along

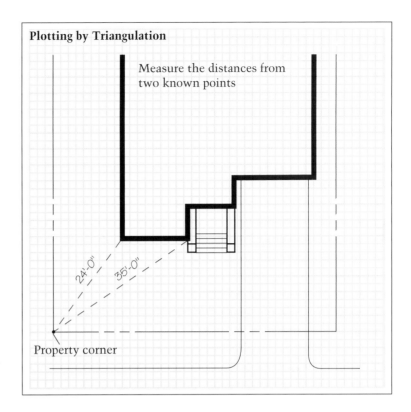

Plotting by Triangulation

Measure the distances from two known points

24'-0"

35'-0"

Property corner

Checklist for Measuring the Site

Your base map will be most useful if it is truly complete. Check the following list to be sure you don't omit anything.
- Water meter
- Site where main water line enters the house (usually in line with the meter)
- Main shutoff valve
- Each side of doors and windows
- Height of windowsills above ground
- Telephone and power lines
- Electric meter
- Downspouts
- Clothes-dryer vent
- Outdoor lights
- Hose bibbs (outdoor faucets)
- Lamp posts
- Telephone poles
- Fences and walls, with gates
- All other structures
- Driveway
- Trees (identify species if possible)
  Trunk diameter
  Canopy diameter
  Height of lowest branch
  Height of crown
- Shrubs (identify species if possible)
- Rock outcroppings
- Banks, cliffs, steep places

the contour. Walk downhill another 5 feet, and use the same method to mark the 10-foot contour. You will use triangulation to indicate the position of each stake on the base map, then you will connect them with appropriate contour lines. For now, mark the approximate position of each stake on the plot plan, take the measurements necessary to complete the triangulation, and record the measurements.

DRAWING THE BASE MAP

Once the measuring is finished, you will draw a base map. Depending on your drafting skills, you can make this more or less finished and professional-looking. If you own and know how to use a T square, drafting board, and other drafting tools, by all means do so. However, the method described here will produce an accurate base map with a minimum of tools or techniques. You will need a pad of 18- × 24-inch graph paper, a roll of 18-inch tracing paper, a 45-degree and a 60-degree triangle, a roll of drafting tape, a compass, an architect's scale, a pencil, a sharpener, and a good eraser.

Select a smooth, hard drawing surface. Tape a piece of drafting paper to it by placing a piece of drafting tape at each corner. (Drafting tape releases easily, unlike the masking tape it resembles.)

Use the architect's scale to measure distances; don't try to count squares on the drafting paper. However, the squares will help you draw horizontal and vertical lines easily.

An architect's scale calibrates automatically to the scale you select, saving much calculation. Select a scale that will allow the finished plan to fit comfortably on the drafting paper you are using. Depending on your lot size, this will probably be ¼ inch = 1 foot, ³⁄₁₆ inch = 1 foot, or ⅛ inch = 1 foot.

Begin by drawing on the paper the baseline from which you began measuring the site. Place it carefully so you will be able to fit all the property lines on the paper. Using your notes, draw the house and the property lines first, then other major features.

To plot a point by using triangulation, set the compass to represent one measurement. Place the point of the compass on the place from which you measured, such as a corner of the house, and draw an arc. Then set the compass to the second measurement and draw another arc. Where the arcs intersect is the point you are trying to locate.

To show trees, draw a small circle to represent the trunk and a larger circle to show the extent of the crown (this larger circle is often called the drip line).

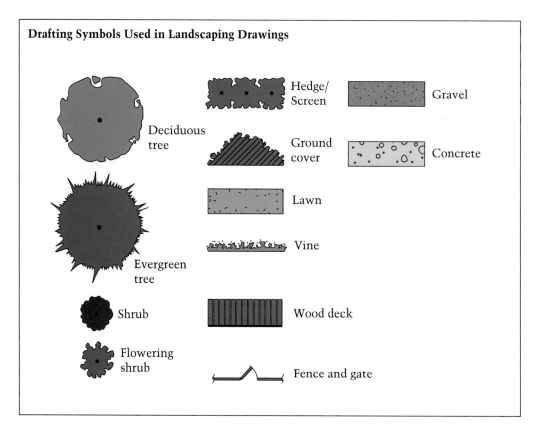

Drafting Symbols Used in Landscaping Drawings

Deciduous tree

Evergreen tree

Shrub

Flowering shrub

Hedge/Screen

Ground cover

Lawn

Vine

Wood deck

Fence and gate

Gravel

Concrete

Base Map

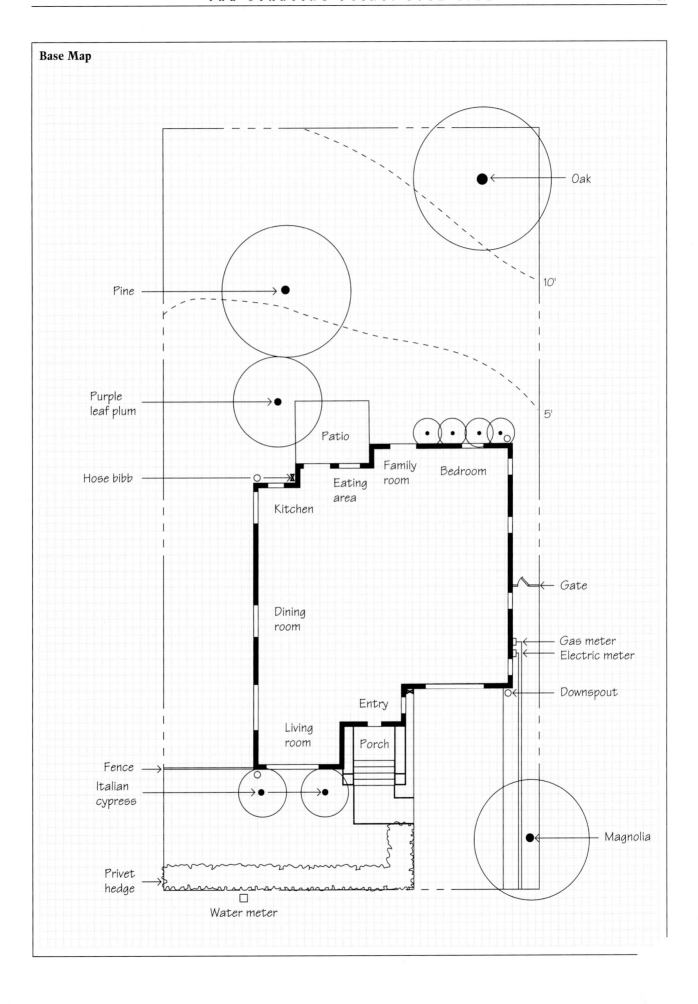

Making Notes on the Plot Plan

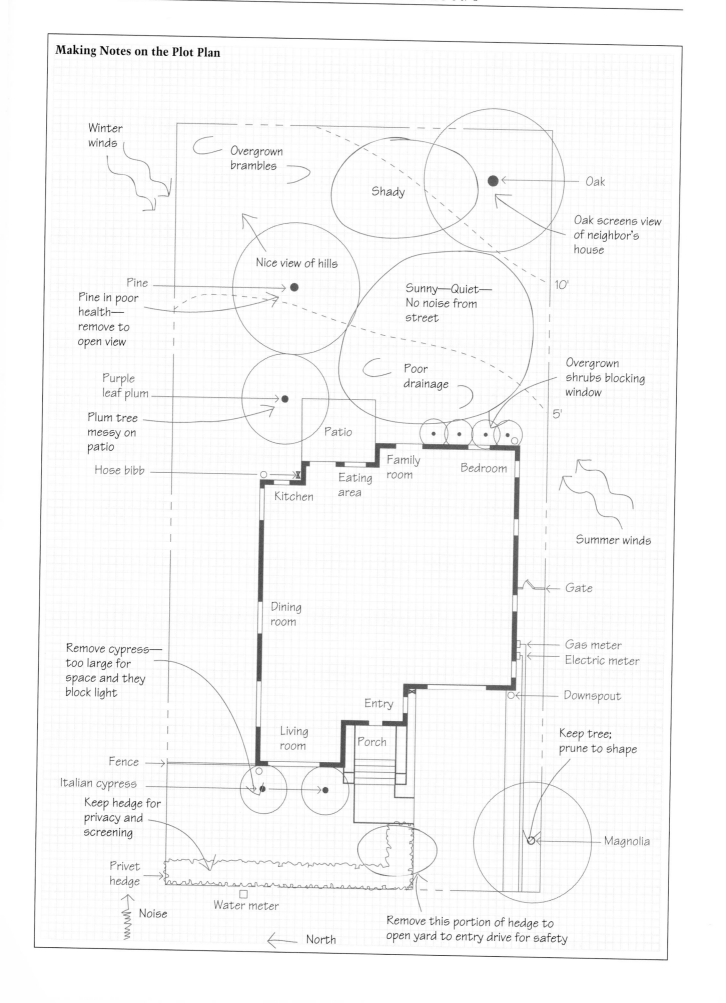

When the map is finished, make several copies. These will be the beginnings of many other plans. If you are mapping contour intervals, put them on one of the copies; this map will be the basis for planning drainage, slope correction, erosion control, and other earth-moving tasks.

ANALYZING YOUR LANDSCAPE

The last step before planning the landscape is analyzing what you have. You will take a close look at the property, think about what you like and don't like, and try to foresee problems.

Walk around the site, taking notes on a copy of the base map. Record the direction of the winter and summer winds and areas that might be too hot in the summer. Note any problem spots, such as places with poor drainage, very rocky or steep areas, or signs of erosion. If there are positive features you want to take full advantage of, such as an attractive rock outcropping, note these, too.

If you are renovating an existing landscape, now is the time to decide what to keep and what to discard. Be conservative at this point, planning to discard only those plants and structures you know you don't want. If you remove something at the beginning of the project, you can't bring it back later.

Large trees are usually valuable assets to a landscape and worth keeping if at all possible. Besides the obvious beauty and value of old, large trees, many cities have "heritage tree" laws that forbid removing them.

Some trees are dangerous, however, and should be removed or repaired. Trees with hollow areas in the trunk or in major branches are weak and may break in a storm. Examine holes in the trunk to see how extensive the hollow is. Major branches that form a narrow angle where they separate from the trunk are also weak. They are not well connected to the trunk and may break. If you have doubts about the safety or health of a tree, ask an arborist to assess it. He or she may recommend removal or tell you how to prune or brace it.

Trees and shrubs that are ugly and overgrown can often be made attractive with proper pruning. Some tangled shrubs conceal a form that has character and interest, and just needs to be revealed. Pruning can "open up" dark and gloomy trees. Pruning large trees can be dangerous, however; leave the work to professionals.

If it appears that the site was attractively landscaped at one time, try to imagine what it looked like when it was cared for. It will be easier—and perhaps more attractive—to plan the new landscape if you incorporate elements from the old one, such as paths and major plantings.

Now you are finished with gathering information and ready to begin the creative process of designing the new landscape.

When analyzing your yard, note your reactions to features as well as their practical aspects. Keep those features that you like, even if it takes a bit more work to figure out how to include them.

Planning Your Landscape

Step-by-step, put together a workable plan, complete with estimates of what it will cost and how long it will take.

Planning a landscape is a creative process. You begin by becoming familiar with the land—which you've already done. Next you assess your family's needs and wants, its likes and dislikes, and gather ideas. Then you put the assessments and ideas together creatively to come up with "solutions" (as landscape architects call them) that result in a finished landscape design. This chapter discusses the assessing and problem-solving parts of the process.

To be creative, you need to be comfortably familiar with all the elements of the situation, you need to concentrate on the problem, and you need to allow yourself enough time. During this planning phase, you will gather yet more information. You'll assemble your information as lists and as sketches on a copy of the plot plan. You'll mull the information as you walk across the yard, trying to solve a problem. Hold off on making final decisions until you're quite sure you have the best plan. Creativity often feels more like a discovery than something you've put together. You might leave a copy of the base map sitting out for a week. One day you will see quite clearly an answer to at least one of the problems, and then another, until the whole layout falls into place. But this "discovery" comes only after much work, and each of the elements of the problem must have time to sink deeply into the mind. Be patient, and the answer will come.

A good landscape plan is developed through a series of steps. The plan shown here is at a stage called bubble drawing, in which basic functions are assigned to parts of the site.

PLANNING GARDEN SPACES

Planning works best if it moves from the most abstract considerations to the most concrete, in a series of steps rather than all at once. Resist the impulse to immediately begin to select specific plants and furnishings. Plant selection is the very last item in planning, and you will do it better if you approach it in several incremental stages.

Make landscape decisions in phases, moving from a generalized scheme to a precise one. Record your decisions on a landscape plan—depending on the phase, you might want a bubble plan, concept drawing, elevation, working plan, or detail plan.

A *bubble plan* is the place to define the major areas. Bubble plans are quick and easy to draw, so they encourage you to experiment and discard until you are sure you have created the best plan possible. Begin with the spaces

that offer the least choice. Perhaps there is only one location where the garbage cans will be accessible from both the street and the kitchen. Indicate it with a "bubble," a rough circle that represents a functional area but does not define its form. For example, you might want to show a sitting area immediately outside some French doors. A bubble defines the rough space the sitting area will occupy, without requiring you to decide if it will be a deck, patio, or lawn.

As you experiment with bubble plans, think about things like the view, the heat of the sun, and the prevailing breezes. Think also about traffic patterns. Routes that will be used frequently should be as short as possible. Show these frequently used traffic patterns with arrows from one bubble to the next. If the arrows are too long, try another arrangement to make access more convenient.

Planning for Easy Maintenance

The amount of time you spend caring for your yard will depend on how you plan it. To keep your maintenance time—and costs—low, follow these pointers:

Avoid having a lawn or keep it small Lawns, with their mowing needs, take more maintenance time than any other type of planting. Low ground covers or mixed plantings are attractive and take less time.

Put deep ground covers under messy trees Raking fallen leaves, a time-consuming task, can be avoided if the leaves sift into a deep ground cover, such as ivy. They become a mulch there, eventually providing nutrients to the trees and ground cover.

Select plants that don't need much work Some plants need regular spraying, staking, pruning, and extra care. Most plants native to your area, or to an area with a similar climate, grow as if they were wild, with little attention from you. As you select plants, ask the nursery staff about the care required.

Keep the design informal Landscape features with soft edges and uneven surfaces take less care than formal ones. For example, informal hedges can be

pruned once a year, but formal hedges with flat surfaces and sharp corners begin to look ragged just a few weeks after shearing. The more like natural scenery your landscape looks, the less you will have to do to keep it looking presentable.

Automate the watering If you live in an area where you need to water regularly, install an irrigation system with a timer. Watering is a time-consuming task in dry climates. A drip or sprinkler system—especially one with a timer—will save many hours of work every summer.

Bubble Plan

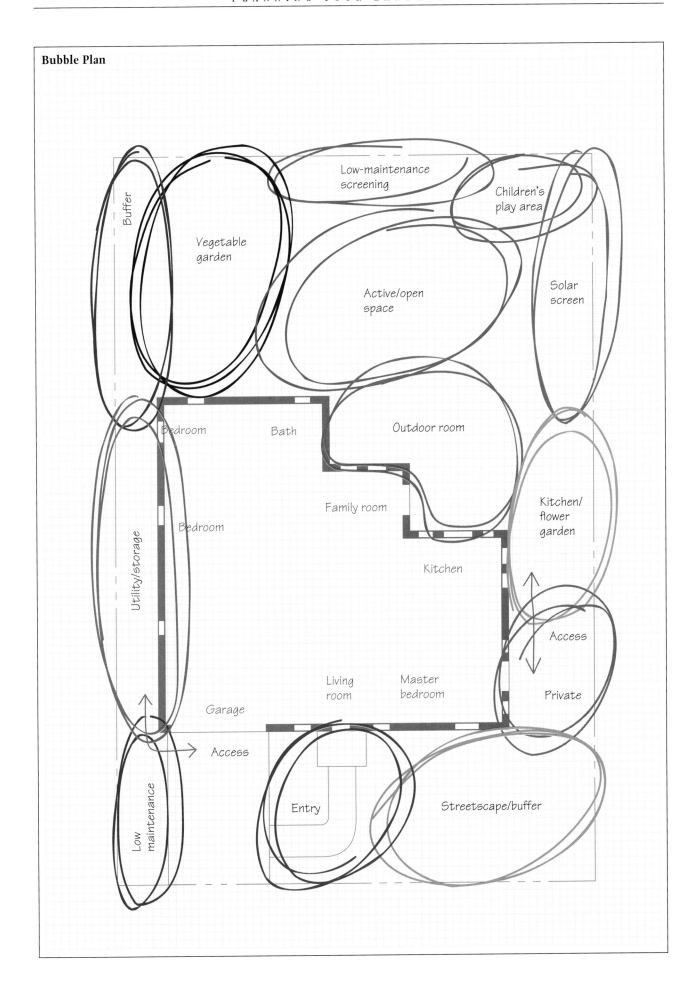

Concept Plan

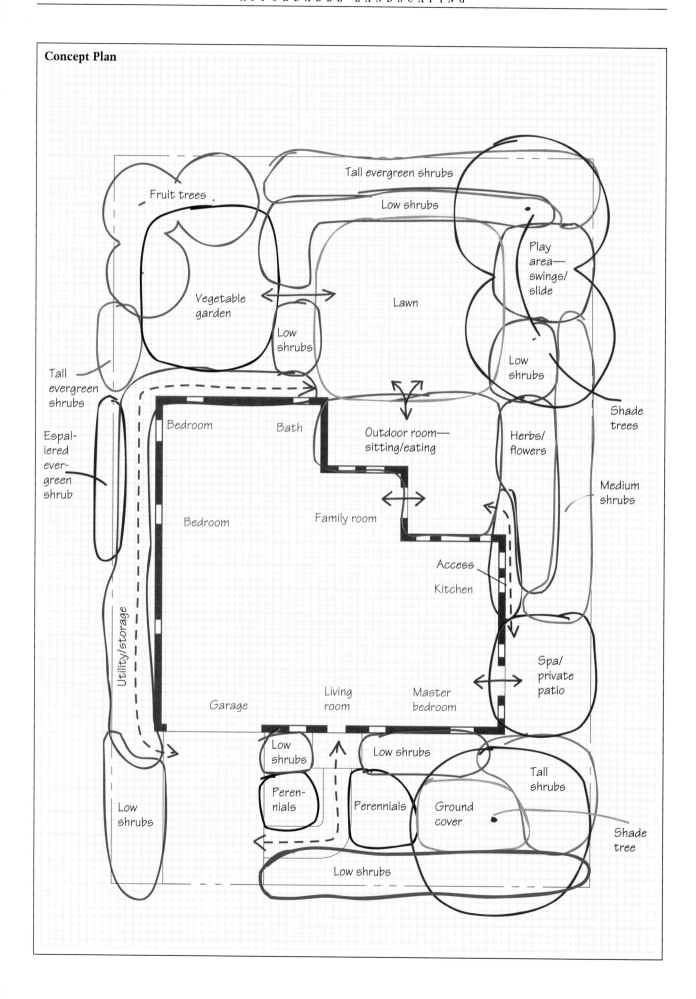

A *concept plan* is more specific than a bubble plan. It shows all the major elements of the landscape: the paving, structures, and masonry work, and the scheme for major plantings.

To continue the preceding example, suppose you decide that the sitting area outside the French doors should be a deck even with the house floor and tied to a patio by two wide steps at lawn level. Since this side of the house faces south and you live in a hot climate, you decide to add some sort of overhead structure to provide shade. These items are noted roughly on the concept plan.

An *elevation* might also help at this stage. Elevations are drawings of the landscape as it would appear from some vantage point, such as the front of the house as seen from the street, rather than from a bird's-eye view. They help you visualize your landscape, to see what it will feel like to be in it and next to it.

Elevations can be simple drawings, or complex constructions. One easy way to make them is to photograph the background (such as the front of the house), make enlarged copies of the photograph, and draw plants and landscape features on the copies.

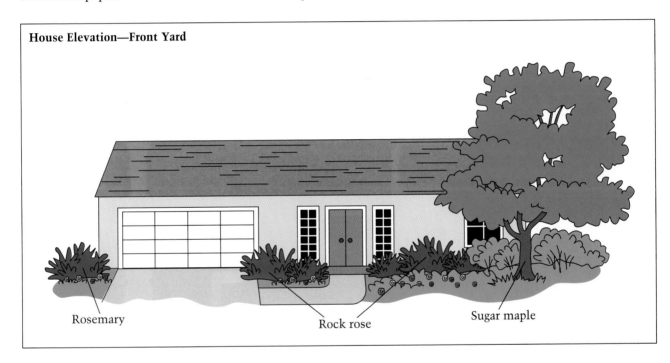

House Elevation—Front Yard

Rosemary

Rock rose

Sugar maple

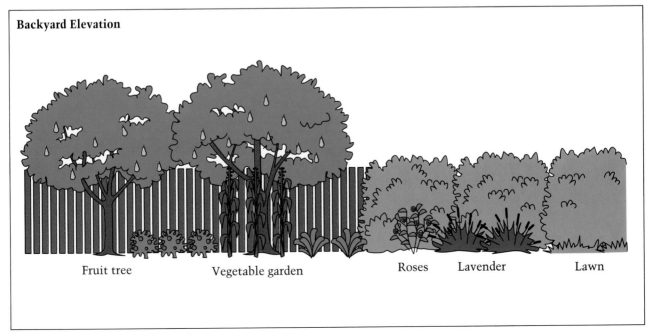

Backyard Elevation

Fruit tree

Vegetable garden

Roses

Lavender

Lawn

Working Plan

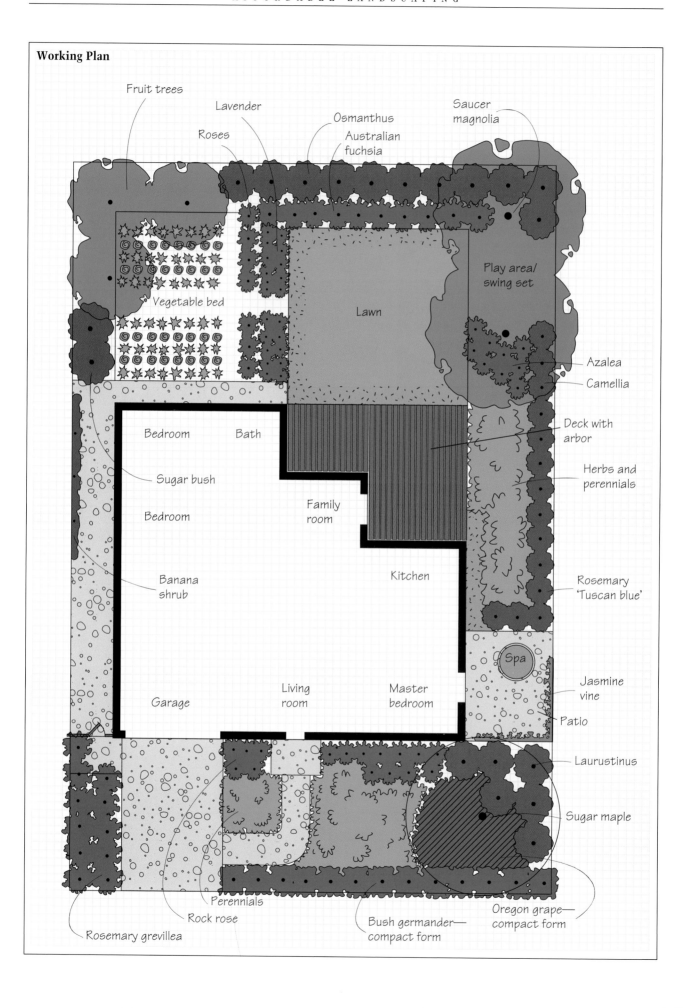

Fruit trees

Lavender

Roses

Osmanthus
Australian
fuchsia

Saucer
magnolia

Play area/
swing set

Vegetable bed

Lawn

Azalea

Camellia

Deck with
arbor

Bedroom   Bath

Sugar bush

Herbs and
perennials

Bedroom

Family
room

Banana
shrub

Kitchen

Rosemary
'Tuscan blue'

Spa

Jasmine
vine

Living
room

Master
bedroom

Garage

Patio

Laurustinus

Sugar maple

Perennials

Rock rose

Bush germander
compact form

Oregon grape
compact form

Rosemary grevillea

A *working plan* is the final plan. Working plans show the exact dimensions of the deck and the patio, the arbor that will provide shade, and the grapevines at the corners of the arbor that will be trained to cover it. The working plan also shows the identity and location of all major plants and ground covers. Several working plans might be made for different phases of the work. One might show grading and drainage; another, the construction; and yet another, the planting.

A *detail drawing* shows more construction details than there is room for on the working plan. In the example given, a detail drawing might specify deck and arbor construction details. The plan would show the dimensions of the lumber, the types of hardware necessary, and the joinery used. Other detail drawings could show the irrigation system, and fence and gate construction.

Making detailed plans forces you to work out all aspects of the construction. The less construction experience you have, the more important making detailed plans is. People experienced in construction are able to work with rough dimensions, doing much of the detail planning mentally. If you are inexperienced with this type of work, however, you will reduce errors if you plan the job on paper in as much detail as possible. Detail plans are also useful for estimating costs and shopping for materials.

In addition, detail plans are often necessary when applying for building permits. Building departments require a permit for the construction of many structures, including decks more than 18 inches above the ground, and walls over 3 feet high. Fences and most sheds don't require permits. If you aren't sure whether a job needs a permit, ask the building department. Make neat, detailed plans of any work that will require a permit.

Considering Style

Some of the thinking that must be done before discovering the final design pertains to the "feel" your landscape will have—its style, the way it fits your house and your neighborhood, and the way it reflects the native ecology.

Style is difficult to define but easy to recognize. It is the characteristic feeling or mood of

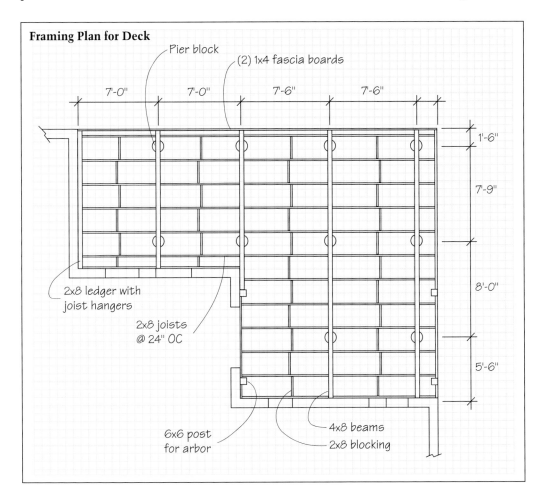

Framing Plan for Deck

Pier block

(2) 1x4 fascia boards

7'-0"   7'-0"   7'-6"   7'-6"

1'-6"

7'-9"

8'-0"

2x8 ledger with joist hangers

2x8 joists @ 24" OC

5'-6"

6x6 post for arbor

4x8 beams

2x8 blocking

*Although not truly
Japanese, this garden
incorporates features
of Japanese design that
give a strong sense
of style. The presence of
water, the natural—
but rigidly controlled—
plant arrangement,
and the ornaments all
contribute to the effect.*

*A Victorian gazebo
highlights the romantic
English style of this
large garden.*

a landscape, and it is often described by a name. For instance, you might have a Victorian garden or an English country garden or even an art deco garden.

Whatever style you pick, execute it consistently. The design will be stronger, and more attractive, when every decision—the way a path curves, the paving material you select for a patio, the plants that surround the lawn— contributes to the overall effect.

One major difference among landscape styles is the degree of formality. Formality is represented in landscaping by straight lines or controlled curves, by a formal balance in which the two sides of a garden mirror one another, and by an emphasis on dense geometric forms, created by pruning, rather than loose organic shapes. Informality is more like untouched nature, with its undefined boundaries, wandering curves, and unrestrained growth.

A natural-style garden re-creates the tallgrass prairie that once covered this part of Wisconsin. It will take little care once it is well established.

Informal planting surrounds a charming garden-shed "cottage."

The landscape style you select should harmonize with your house. It doesn't need to be exactly the same style, but landscape style shouldn't conflict with house style. For instance, if your house is a Victorian with lots of porches and gingerbread, you could plan a Victorian garden, with shaped flower beds and dramatic plantings. But an informal English country garden, with a profusion of flowers in delightful disarray, would also harmonize with the style of the house. A starkly modern landscape, however, would not. Whatever you

This patio gives a comfortable sense of enclosure. Its low fence and shrubbery define the space and add a feeling of security without blocking the view.

choose, it should be something you like and will be happy living with.

Consider also the style of your neighborhood. Probably your home is adjacent to at least two other homes. The eye doesn't stop at property lines; it views the yards as a unit. If the style of your yard clashes with those of your neighbors' yards, all three will look less attractive, no matter how pleasant each might be by itself.

Another "neighborhood" to consider is the natural ecology of your region, with its climate, topography, and plant communities. If you harmonize with nature, not only will your plantings seem to blend into the greater scheme of life, but your landscape will be easier to care for. Plants that are native to your area, or to a region with a similar climate, are easier to care for than imports. Often natives need no special care at all. They can be planted and then enjoyed as if they were growing in the wild.

Considering Function

A particularly important part of landscape planning involves meeting your family's needs. Garden space is used in one of three ways: to live in, to do something with, or to look at. Decks and patios are living spaces, just as if they were rooms of the house. You eat and converse there, and parties spill out of the house and onto them. Vegetable gardens, sandboxes,

and boat storage pads are functional spaces, designed for practical use. The front of your house is probably to be looked at; it is designed to be attractive from the street and to visitors as they approach the front entry.

Outdoor "rooms" Landscape designers think of garden living areas as if they were rooms of a house, with floors, walls, and ceilings. The paving or lawn underfoot makes the floor, and the ceiling is tree branches or overhead structures. The walls may be the house walls, fences, low hedges—anything that defines the space and gives a feeling of enclosure.

The degree of enclosure contributes to the feeling of a space. Too much enclosure is oppressive; too little makes you feel exposed. Most people enjoy a space that is defined but open, and has a view. A deck with a low railing that overlooks a wide lawn is such a space.

The use to which a garden "room" will be put should define its size. A private patio off a master bedroom should be intimate, with just enough room for a couple of chairs and a small table. A deck intended to extend a living room should be designed to the same scale as the living room and connected to it with generous doors. It should be large enough to hold several chairs and tables, with room between them for easy traffic circulation.

Top: A patio or deck can extend your home, creating an appealing place to relax, visit, or eat.
Bottom: A carefully worked out design, this formal French-style garden is intended to be enjoyed from an upstairs window.

Plan your outdoor living areas as if they were rooms of your house. A patio outside a kitchen might be designed for outdoor eating, with a table and benches, a barbecue, and perhaps a cabinet for storing tableware, as in a dining room. A children's play area should be designed to be like a child's room, with ample toy storage that is low and easy to get to. It should be safe and secure, so young children can be left alone without parental concern.

Outdoor "paintings"   Parts of the yard that are meant to be viewed can be thought of as landscape paintings. One kind of "vista" area is an open space that is to be crossed, such as a front yard. Such areas are best designed by standing at the most usual viewing point and imagining the landscape as it will look from there. Another area meant to be viewed is a courtyard too small for sitting or for a practical use but that can serve as a "picture" to be viewed through a window. Backdrops for lawns or swimming pools might also be designed to be looked at.

Functional areas are often hidden from sight so they can be practical without any concern for their appearance. The garden element that hides them might be attractive, however. A garbage area, for example, can be hidden by a trellis-topped wooden fence, with a clematis

trailing and draping over it. Some functional areas can be interesting or even beautiful without detracting from their practical use. A vegetable garden, if kept neat, can be an attractive edge for a lawn or an interesting conversation piece next to a patio.

Consider the space at your disposal and try to match it to your family's wish list. You may want to start planning with functional necessities, such as garbage storage and dog runs, and then add the desirable extras. Spend some time gathering ideas. Talk to friends, read magazines and books about landscaping, visit garden shows, and observe other people's yards to get ideas of what you would like in yours.

Considering Natural Elements

The amount of sun, shade, and wind your landscape receives should influence your choice of plantings and structures.

Light and shade   The brightness and quality of light form a backdrop to all human activity. It isn't always noticed, but the quality of light affects the beauty of a place and the comfort we feel in it. In general, we enjoy light shade in hot weather and warm sun in cool weather.

Overhead structures are immediate but expensive ways to shade an area. Trees are not so expensive but take years to grow large enough to cast significant shade. Compromise by building a temporary structure—perhaps a light frame covered with split bamboo window shades or with canvas. At the same time, plant a tree. By the time the bamboo or canvas begins to weather and look ragged, the tree will have grown enough to shade the area.

Deciduous trees are often the best choices for shade. They block the sun in the summer,

---

Some Family Needs

Your ideal landscape will meet the most important of your family's needs. To be sure you don't overlook possible uses of your space, review this list.

Outdoor Living Areas
Patio or deck
Outdoor eating area
Outdoor cooking area
Private garden
Secluded reading nook
Sunbathing area
View point

Children's Play Areas
Sandbox
Lawn
Playhouse
Treehouse
Swing set/climbing structure
Wading pool
Racetrack for tricycles
Platform

Recreation Areas
Game court: Tennis, basketball, handball, horseshoes, volleyball
Game lawn: Croquet, putting green, bowling
Exercise circuit
Swimming pool
Spa or hot tub

Utility Areas
Garbage cans
Dog run or doghouse
Firewood storage
RV or boat storage
Storage shed
Potting shed
Composting area
Extra parking

Specialty Gardens
Vegetable garden
Cutting garden
Herb garden
Garden pool
Rock garden

Dappled shade makes this corner of the garden an ideal setting for a quiet retreat.

when we need shade, and let it through in the winter, when the sun is welcome. A deciduous tree planted so it shades your home can reduce both heating and cooling bills. Evergreen trees have a place in landscaping, but they don't make good shade trees. Not only do they shade in the winter, when you would like the sun, but most evergreens cast deep shade, which can be gloomy and will discourage plants.

The house itself affects the quality of light. The wall facing south reflects sunlight and heat, making the area before it oppressively hot in the summer and deliciously warm in cold weather. This is a good location for a spring-and-fall sunning patio, especially if you can plan some windbreaks to keep the wind from chilling the area. If you want to cool the south wall, plant a shade tree in front of it or cover it with vines, perhaps on a trellis.

The sun never touches the north wall. In the summer, it is a haven for shade-loving plants and is the cool spot for hot-weather lounging. In the winter, however, it is cold and damp. If you want to use the area in cool weather, avoid establishing anything that obstructs light on the north side.

The east wall receives morning light, but is shielded from hot afternoon sun. It is an ideal place for growing delicate flowers. The west wall gets the hottest afternoon sun and often needs some shade to protect it.

Most plants like as much light as they can get, but need some protection from oppressive sun. Many plants grow well under the protecting skirt of a tree, where they receive direct sun early and late in the day, but are shaded at midday. Heat-loving, summer-blooming flowers do well on the south side of shrubs, trees, and structures. Cool-weather flowers often do best on the north or east sides.

Overhead structures used for shade are generally more cool and pleasant if they are open rather than solid, allowing air circulation. Also, the pattern of broken sunlight cast by a lattice structure or a vine on an arbor is attractive and adds to the pleasure of using the space.

Wind Effective windbreaks are tall but not solid. Solid structures, such as board fences or buildings, deflect wind, which then swirls around them. A line of trees or a lattice fence, however, slows the wind without deflecting it, making a more effective windbreak.

If wind is severe, plan a windbreak of fast-growing trees on the windward side of your property. A few large shrubs around a sitting area create a pocket of warmth.

SOLVE SOIL PROBLEMS FIRST

When you install your landscape, you will begin with the soil. This is a good place to begin planning, too. Think of soil problems—those that involve drainage or erosion—as you work with your first bubble drawings. If the problems are severe, plan their solution first, unencumbered by other considerations. Begin bubble drawings after the soil problems are solved.

Plan Ahead

Solving soil problems involves moving soil. To help you plan soil movement, put a piece of tracing paper over your contour map and draw in changes you need to make in the contours. Studying sections—cross-sections of ground where you will be cutting or filling—can also help you plan earth movement.

Calculating the Volume of Cuts and Fills

A simple way to estimate the volume of soil to be cut or filled is to make a grid over the areas on the plan where soil is to be moved. Either draw a grid on an overlay, or use tracing paper with a grid printed on it. Make the grid in any convenient size, from 1-foot squares to 10-foot squares.

Outline any area where the depth of the soil will be altered by at least 6 inches. Count the squares that are at least halfway within that contour line. Within the contour, outline any area where the depth of the soil that will be cut or filled is at least 1½ feet. Count the squares within that contour. Continue if you are cutting or filling more, with contours at 2½ feet, 3½ feet, and so on. Count the squares within each contour.

Now add up all the counts. If your grid was made of 1-foot squares, you will have the volume in cubic feet of soil. If the grid was of 5- by 5-foot squares (covering 25 square feet), multiply by 25 to get the cubic feet of soil.

Divide the number of cubic feet by 27 to convert to cubic yards. Each cubic yard is approximately one load for a pickup truck.

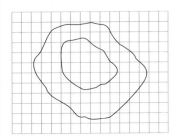

1 grid square = 1 square ft

74 squares in 6" contour
<u>19 squares in 1½-ft contour</u>
93 squares = 93 cubic ft of
          soil

93 ÷ 27 = 3.4 cubic yd

If possible, plan cuts and fills—places where earth is removed and places where it is added—so you don't have to either purchase or dispose of soil. Soil is expensive, and when you purchase it, you take a chance of importing weeds or diseases that weren't there before. Disposing of excess soil also presents problems; you could spend many hours trying to locate a site to dump a few yards of soil.

Try to plan a use for soil you excavate. If you don't need soil to fill low spots or raised beds,

perhaps the excess soil can be used as a slight mound in a new lawn or flower bed. Mounds are attractive if they look natural; plan them to be low in proportion to their width, with edges tapered very gently into the surrounding topography. Be sure, however, that you will not be interfering with the surface drainage; your mound should not become a dam.

Solving Drainage Problems

Surface drainage allows water to run downhill to an acceptable disposal site, such as a storm sewer or drainage ditch. As you move soil around, be careful not to create low spots that will catch water and interfere with the surface drainage. Be particularly careful not to interfere with the drainage of water away from your house. To carry water away from the house and prevent its filling your basement, the land around the house should slope gently down in all directions.

Persistent wet spots, or signs that some areas have stayed wet for a long time, signify drainage problems. The soil in those spots can't absorb water as fast as it is arriving. This might be because too much water is flowing for any soil to absorb, or because the soil drains too slowly to absorb even moderate amounts of water. To solve such drainage problems, use one of the three approaches that follow.

Top: The soil excavated for the pool was used to create a low mound that makes the sitting area more private and also introduces a vertical dimension to an otherwise flat yard. Bottom: Areas that accumulate water can often be drained just by altering the slope of the ground.

Slope Ground Away From House

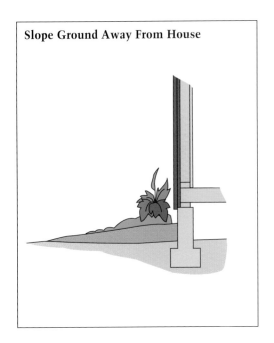

The first approach to solving drainage problems is to slope the land so water flows gently off the property. By moving soil from high places to fill low spots, you can moderate the slope of the ground so rainwater will be directed to a disposal site instead of settling in low spots.

Another approach to improving drainage is to increase the ability of the soil to absorb water. Use this approach when you can't get rid of low spots that collect water—the land may be too level to drain, or impossible to shape for drainage. You'll need to make the low spot as level as possible, to spread out the water that must be absorbed. Then you will dig ample quantities of organic matter into the soil, as deeply as possible. See page 82 for instructions.

A third approach to drainage problems is to drain the water away with drain lines. This approach is useful for drainage problems caused by water seepage from the ground. Such seepage might be from a natural spring or high water table, or it might come from the yards of uphill neighbors who overwater their lawns. Modern drain lines are flexible corrugated pipes, 3 or 4 inches in diameter, pierced with rows of holes to let water enter them. They are laid in a ditch under the wet spot to collect water and carry it off the property. For instructions on installing drain lines, see page 62.

To plan a drain line, first decide where to empty it. Drain lines must run downhill from where the water enters them into a lower spot. The slope of the drain line must be at least 1 foot of fall for every 100 feet of run (or about $\frac{1}{8}$

inch of fall per foot of run). In urban settings, drain lines often empty into a street gutter, which drains into a storm sewer. In such a setting, you might have to put the drain line under the sidewalk.

Next, decide where the water will enter the drain line. If, when you dig into a wet spot, water flows from the soil to fill the hole, your problem comes from a high water table. To lower a high water table, you must place the drain line deeper than the wet spot. It will lower the water table to the depth of the bottom of the drain line. If you intend to plant a lawn on the site, a drain line 1 to 2 feet deep is sufficient. If you want to plant a tree, the line should be 3 to 4 feet deep.

If the wet area is wider than 50 feet, plan a network of drain lines under it. Place lines about 50 feet apart in sandy soil that drains quickly. Place them about 25 feet apart in clay soil that drains slowly.

If the wet spot is on the side of a hill or right at its base, the water is flowing down the hill

Drain lines, which are laid in ditches and then covered with soil or gravel, carry water from wet spots to a disposal site.

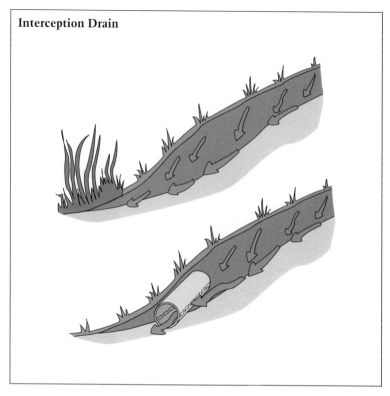

Interception Drain

On a sloping site, low retaining walls slow the flow of runoff and provide more gardening space. The end of a drain line is visible in the lowest wall.

through the soil. Plan a drain line across the hillside, a few feet above the wet spot. By intersecting the stream of water, you will be able to drain it away before it reaches the surface.

Dealing With Hillsides and Banks

Steep hillsides present three problems: The soil might erode, it might slip, and the steep land has limited utility. If much of your property is steep, or if you want to use all of it, the best solution is terracing, a series of level areas held in place by retaining walls. Terraces require a great deal of labor to install, and are often located where it is difficult to work with power equipment, so the digging must be done by hand. However, once completed, terraces can be beautiful and interesting, and they make available parts of the yard that would otherwise be used only to grow ground cover.

Plan each terrace so that the soil dug out of the hillside is used behind that terrace's retaining wall; this avoids moving soil very far. Keep the retaining walls as low as possible. If a wall is less than 3 feet high and there is a lot of room behind it, so it can have considerable backward slope, it can be made of pieces of broken sidewalk or native stone, which are often available at no cost. For instructions on building retaining walls, see page 62.

Landslides or land slippage are likely only in certain areas. They are caused by steep land underlaid by a clay subsoil. Water percolating through the topsoil collects at the interface with the subsoil and makes a slippery layer there, causing the topsoil to slip or slump. If your hillside is on bedrock, as many hillsides are, there is little danger of it slipping. Ask the neighbors if land slippage is a problem in your area. The building department can also provide information.

Land slippage can usually be prevented with a retaining wall at the base of the slope. Since the wall will be holding back many tons of soil, it should be professionally installed. It must be very deep, strong, and well anchored.

Simple erosion control is based on keeping rainwater from running over the surface of the soil by slowing it down enough that it has time to sink in. Covering the soil with a mulch, or with a coarse fabric made for this purpose, accomplishes this immediately. Fibrous mulches, such as shredded bark or pine needles, stay in place on steep ground better than particulate mulch. The mulch should be a couple of inches deep and cover the soil completely. Erosion-control fabric should be pegged down with wire staples to keep it from slipping down the hill. For more information on mulches, see page 87.

Top: Erosion-control fabric is a coarse material made of jute. Plants can be placed in holes made in the fabric, which will rot away in a couple of years. To make it more presentable, cover the fabric with a thin mulch.
Bottom: Retaining walls, such as this one made of old railroad ties, keep the ground from slipping or washing onto the lawn below. A wall this high holds back tons of soil; it should be professionally engineered.

Neither mulches nor fabric will last more than a couple of years. For the long term, plan to plant the hillside with a tightly knit ground cover. Vines or plants that lie directly on the soil are the most effective. Ground covers take a couple of years to cover the soil, so they are often used in combination with a mulch, which provides initial protection.

PLANNING HARDSCAPE

Hardscape is a landscaper's term for anything constructed from building materials. It includes structures, retaining walls, paved paths, patios, and fences. These are usually the most expensive parts of a landscape.

As you decide how to provide the "walls," "floors," and "ceilings" of your functional areas, you can incorporate major savings. A satisfactory and attractive outdoor living area can be made of a floor of rolled aggregate with an azalea border and a flowering cherry overhead. Alternatively, it might have a paving of broken sidewalk with creeping mint filling the cracks, a border of mixed flowers, and a Chinese pistachio (*Pistacia chinensis*) or thornless honeylocust (*Gleditsia triacanthos*) for shade. The same area built as a deck with benches, a low railing, and an arbor would cost 10 times as much and take 3 times as long to make.

Made of bricks laid in sand, this patio is relatively inexpensive because of its small size.

Beginning on page 54, you will find information about how to save money when you buy building materials and how to build with them. The sections that follow will discuss the merits and costs of different types of paving and structure, to help you plan the most economical design.

Paving Materials

Paving refers to any material laid on the ground. It may be loose, like gravel; in pieces, like brick; or a monolithic mass, like concrete.

In the following discussion of the costs of different materials, the dollar amounts are relative measures; costs vary. You won't find these prices exactly, but you can use them for comparison purposes. The relationship among them will remain about the same.

Aggregate   As used here, *aggregate* refers to crumbled rock in a variety of particle sizes. The kind of aggregate that makes effective paving contains quite a lot of dust-sized pieces, often called *fines*. (In contrast to paving aggregate, aggregate used for making concrete is cleaner, without fines.) According to locale, paving aggregate might be called bank-run gravel, decomposed granite, shale, decomposed bluestone, or several other names. Because the small particles fill the spaces between the large particles, aggregate compacts solidly to make a surface that looks and feels like packed earth underfoot. Unlike earth, however, it doesn't get muddy when wet, and it doesn't support weed growth. Aggregate is long-lasting and easy to install and care for. When properly installed, it is informal but attractive. An aggregate patio costs about 35 cents per square foot.

Gravel   Also called ornamental rock, gravel is sold under many different names, such as drain rock, pea gravel, or dolomite. All are composed of small pieces of rock. Some are rounded and smooth, others broken and rough. The difference between aggregate and gravel is that gravel contains no fines. Gravel is often graded so all the particles are the same size. This keeps it from compacting; it remains loose. Before selecting a gravel, walk across a sample. Pea gravel, which is composed of small rounded pebbles, feels like loose sand underfoot. It is difficult to walk on, especially in high heels, but soft to fall on. It is a good choice for a children's play area. At the other end of the roughness spectrum, crushed rock is made of broken pieces of rock. Its edges are rough and flat and lock together. It feels like concrete underfoot, and hurts when you fall on it. Decorative gravel costs about 50 cents per square foot.

Broken sidewalk This material is often available free in cities, where construction crews dig up large amounts of it. It is 4 inches thick and in irregular pieces. When it is used as paving, the spaces between pieces can be filled with soil and planted with "crack" plants, such as creeping thyme (*Thyrus serpyllum*) or chamomile (*Chamaemelum nobile*), both of which release a fragrance when stepped on. Because of its thickness and strength, broken sidewalk can be laid directly on soil or a bed of sand or gravel. Hauling it may be difficult—it's heavy.

Brick, stone, and tile Natural stone paving—slate, flagstone, and the like—can be beautiful, but it is usually quite expensive. Flagstone laid on a concrete bed, for instance, costs about $3 per square foot. Brick or concrete pavers laid on sand also cost about $3 per square foot. Some manufactured paving materials are less expensive.

Concrete Fairly inexpensive and very durable, concrete must be skillfully finished to be attractive. If you do the work yourself, it will cost about $1.50 per square foot, compared to about $5.00 per square foot if you have it installed by a professional.

Decks

The construction of a simple deck is within the skills of most people comfortable with woodworking tools. One advantage of a deck over a patio is that it can be at the same level as the floor of the house, so it becomes an extension of the room to which it connects. A patio can be at floor level only if the house has a slab floor, and even then it might require some fill to build it up to the appropriate height. A simple deck costs about $6 per square foot.

Because it can be raised to the same level as the floor of the house, a deck is a natural extension of the indoor living space.

A garden shed placed on skids or simply set on rocks, as is this one, is considered a temporary structure in most localities and doesn't require a building permit.

SELECTING PLANTS

Approach plant selection in steps, as you did landscape planning. Begin by defining what you want a particular plant or planting to do. The more specific you are, the easier it will be to select the plants. On a concept plan, write down the specifications for each planting. Include the sun exposure of the location; any soil problems; how big you want the plant to get; whether it should be deciduous or evergreen; what shape it should be; and anything special about it, such as whether it should have fragrant flowers, not drop fruit (because it will shade a patio), or provide some food crop.

This may be a good place to ask for help. Your two best sources of plant selection help are garden centers and the county cooperative extension office. Cooperative extension agents, in particular, are experts in the plant problems in your region, and their offices often publish lists of especially successful landscape plants. You can find them in county office listings in your telephone book.

Overheads

Shade structures vary in complexity, from a simple framework that supports a vine to an elaborate construction. A simple arbor strong enough to support a heavy vine costs about $8 per square foot.

Sheds

These can be simple potting tables or elaborate garden sheds with storage and work areas. Children's playhouses are sheds with a little extra decoration. If you build a shed on a permanent foundation, you will need to get a building permit. In most areas, structures built on 4 by 4 skids are considered temporary and don't require a permit. Shed construction is the same as house construction, with a foundation, joists, framed walls and roof, siding, and roofing. A simple storage shed, with a floor, roof and four walls, costs about $10 per square foot.

Fences and Walls

All but the most elaborate fences can be constructed by a person comfortable with tools. Walls, depending on their material, can be much more expensive and difficult to erect. A 6-foot-high solid redwood fence costs about $14 per lineal foot; a 3-foot picket fence will run about $5 per lineal foot.

How to Make the Best Choices

If you'd like to make the final selections yourself, here are some rules of thumb to help avoid mistakes.

•Select plants adapted to your climate. A plant native to your area or to a part of the world with a similar climate will need little or no supplemental water. It will need no protection from the cold and only occasional—not routine—spraying to keep it healthy.

•Select plants adapted to their location in your garden. Know the soil and sun conditions to which the plant will be exposed. If the location receives hot afternoon sun, be sure the plants you select for that spot will tolerate the heat. If the area drains poorly, or has sandy soil, or is shaded, select plants that tolerate those conditions. There are plants that will grow and thrive in just about any garden location, but no plant will do well in a location to which it isn't adapted.

•Select plants for their mature size. Buying trees is like buying puppies. They stay small and cute for only a little while, then you live with the full-grown adults for many years. That chubby little evergreen you select to stand beside the front door can develop into a behemoth that will threaten to push the eaves off the house in a few years. Give the plant room

A crabapple is beautiful in the spring, when it is in full bloom, but the fruit creates a mess in the fall. Before making a final decision on your landscape plants, be sure to investigate whether they have such disadvantages.

to grow. If you are concerned about your landscape looking bare while you wait for plants to grow, select temporary "filler" plants. For example, if you are planning to have a maple as a lawn tree, plant it in a group of fast-growing shrubs. The shrubs will give some substance and character to that part of the lawn for a few years. When the maple is large enough to take over its role as a lawn tree, remove the shrubs.

•Ask about "bad habits." Some plants—especially trees—that are splendid in many respects have a single bad trait that can outweigh all their good points. They may have weak crotches that break in storms, bark or fruit that drops to litter the ground beneath them, shallow roots that push up sidewalks or show in the lawn, a vulnerability to a common insect, or leaves that stain concrete.

Selecting Lawn Grass

Ask your local cooperative extension agent to recommend a turfgrass variety for your location. Be sure to explain what kind of use it will get and whether it will be in the sun or shade. The agent may recommend a mix of different grasses, especially if parts of the lawn are sunny and parts shady. The grasses in the mix that are suited to each environment will eventually crowd out the less adapted ones.

For economy, plan to sow grass seed instead of installing sod—it will create just as satisfactory a lawn, but more slowly. However, some grasses, especially those adapted to the South, are only available in sprigs or plugs, and must be purchased that way. Sprigs are short pieces of live grass stems. Plugs are small pieces of sod that you plant at intervals; they will slowly fill in the whole lawn.

Saving Money on Plants

Although you are still in the planning phase of your landscape, you can start thinking of ways to save money on the plants themselves. As you plan, consider specifying smaller, rather than larger, plants. And, depending on your time frame, you may be able to start growing some plants on your own, totally avoiding the need to buy them from a nursery or placing an advance order with a nursery.

Most nurseries and some garden centers propagate their own plants or buy liners—started plants in tiny containers. They transplant the small plants to larger pots; feed, water, and train them until they outgrow their pots; then transplant them again and care for them for months or years more until they are ready to be transplanted again. By the time a tree is 10 feet high, has a trunk 3 inches in

Most of the plants in this new landscape were purchased in 1-gallon cans. The larger trees at the corner and by the entry add some structure to the new landscape and keep it from looking too bare for the first few years.

diameter, and is growing in a 15-gallon can, it has received many hours of care over several years of growth.

It's easy to understand that the nursery must charge a great deal to realize a profit on its investment. A pin oak in a 1-gallon can might cost $5; the same pin oak in a 5-gallon can may cost $30. In a 15-gallon can, it is worth $100. As a 15-foot tree in a 3-foot by 3-foot wooden box, it can cost $300 or more.

Smaller plants are not only less expensive to purchase, but are easier to handle and to plant. They get established more easily and grow more quickly than larger plants. Plants from 1-gallon cans can catch up with plants that were in 5-gallon cans in two or three years. However, a landscape planted with tiny plants looks barren and empty for the first few years. Landscape designers usually place a few large plants in conspicuous places to give a finished look to the landscape immediately, then fill in with smaller plants.

You can fill in the landscape just as quickly and less expensively by planting a temporary landscape between the small plants of your permanent landscape. One type of temporary landscape is a flowering meadow. For just a few dollars, you can buy enough wildflower seeds to fill empty areas with flowers. Broadcast the seeds in the fall or spring, scratch them into the soil with a rake, and water during dry weather. The planted area will be spectacular the first spring and summer. Only a few species

return the second year, but in greater profusion than the first. By the end of the second year, your permanent landscape will be assuming some character of its own, and you can cut down the temporary meadow.

Growing your own plants is the least expensive way to acquire them. In about a year, you can have a number of plants large enough to be installed in your landscape. You can grow your own either from seed or from cuttings.

Seed specialists—see the list on page 92—sell the seeds of countless landscape plants that can be started from seed. If your only experience starting seeds is with vegetables or annual flowers, buy a reliable book about starting landscape plants from seed and follow directions carefully.

It isn't difficult to root a cutting from most hedges or shrubs, although most trees can't be propagated this way. Depending on the season, hedges or shrub cuttings can be rooted and ready to plant in a few weeks to a few months. A small propagation operation in a sunny window can save hundreds of dollars in plant costs.

See the list on page 92 for books that will help you get started propagating and growing your own plants.

Some Nice Touches

Most fragrant plants are best enjoyed at close range, so plan to plant them next to a walk or by a door. Don't forget plants with fragrant leaves. You can pluck a leaf from a laurel (*Laurus nobilis*) shrub as you pass and enjoy its fragrance as you walk to the car. Fragrant ground covers planted in cracks in a patio or path, or allowed to trail over a path from the edges, release their fragrance as you tread on them. A third—and especially nice—touch with fragrant plants is to place a daphne (*Daphne cneorum*) in an enclosed nook or small patio. Daphne is one of the few plants with a fragrance strong enough to fill an area with its perfume. That corner will be awash in scent for a couple of weeks in the spring.

Other candidates for close-up locations are plants you are especially fond of. Put your favorite flowers close by the front door just outside the kitchen window, or next to a favorite patio chair—wherever they can be seen and enjoyed frequently and at close range.

Spring bulbs erupt from the ground as a welcome surprise in the spring. They are an even greater delight if they are planted in unexpected places: under ground covers, in perennial borders that will still be bare when the bulbs appear, and in large containers that hold shrubs or small trees.

Edible ornamentals (see page 50) add a new aspect of sensory pleasure to the garden: taste. Some ornamental plants bear edible fruit and some food plants are beautiful enough to include in the landscape. Alpine strawberries (*Fragaria vesca* 'Semperflorens'), for instance, are excellent border plants because they don't grow runners, and children love to search for the sweet "wild" strawberries. In the Middle Ages, carrots were valued for the ornamental value of their feathery foliage. They are wonderful garden accents or companions for flowers—at least until you pull and eat them.

Hummingbirds and butterflies are delightful garden ornaments. They can be encouraged to visit by planting flowers that attract them (see page 50).

Indicate all your plant selections on one copy of your working plan.

PLANNING IRRIGATION SYSTEMS

Once you know what plants are going where, you can plan your irrigation system. Read about irrigation system installation (see page 76) before you plan yours.

All gardens should have some sort of irrigation system. How complex and expensive a system depends on how much watering you expect to do.

There are three types of irrigation systems: hose-end systems, sprinkler systems, and drip systems. Each has its own benefits and drawbacks. Most yards use at least two, and sometimes all three types, to meet the water needs of different areas. For example, a hose will do for trees or shrubs that don't usually need watering, but might during dry spells; a drip system is best for vegetable gardens, flower borders, and shrubs that need regular watering; and lawns and ground covers should be watered with a sprinkler system.

Designing a Hose-End System

A few faucets in the yard doesn't seem like a "system." Thinking of them as a system, however, makes watering easier. If you water only during occasional droughts, a few faucets are

all you need. Such a system is less expensive and easier to install than either of the other systems, and can water anything in the garden.

A hose-end system consists of a few hose bibbs (outdoor faucets with hose threads on the end) strategically placed around the landscape, a hose to attach to each of the faucets, and nozzles for each hose. Plan the hose bibbs so a 50-foot length of hose will reach from one of them to any place in the garden you want water—it's easier to dig a ditch and put a hose bibb at the back of the lawn one time than to drag 150 feet of hose back there from the house hundreds of times over the years. Plan to provide, at each bibb, a reel to store the hose and a place to store nozzles. These refinements will make a world of difference in how easy watering will be.

Some hose bibbs are probably already in place next to the house; this is the beginning of your system. Decide which one the rest of the lines will be attached to. Then plan ditches for the pipes from each bibb location to the

A frost-heaved and broken concrete patio becomes an asset with the addition of wooly thyme (Thymus pseudolanuginosus) *growing in the crack. Wooly thyme is tough enough to tolerate foot traffic and releases a delightful fragrance when trod upon.*

attachment point. Plan carefully to make each ditch as short as possible. Avoid sidewalks, driveways, trees, and shrubs if you can. It's possible to tunnel through tree roots and go under walks up to about 6 feet wide, but it's difficult (see page 77). Where possible, run ditches next to walks, foundations, or fence lines, to protect the water lines from any digging or tilling that might take place over them.

Indicate all your decisions on your plan, making an overlay if necessary.

Designing a Sprinkler System

Sprinklers are the best systems for covering an area evenly with water. The most expensive systems to install, they are the least trouble to operate. If you need to water regularly or frequently during the summer, install one for the lawn and ground cover areas, which will need even watering. Although they have a reputation for wasting water, a well-designed and properly operated sprinkler system can be almost as efficient as a drip system.

Begin planning a sprinkler system by looking under "Irrigation" in the classified pages of your telephone book. Find listings for parts suppliers. A supplier will give you a catalog to work with and will help you plan the system. If you decide to do the planning yourself, have a supplier check your finished plan.

Your next task is to determine the flow rate at a hose bibb. Draw a line at the gallon level of a bucket and place it under a hose bibb. With a stopwatch, measure the number of seconds it takes to fill the bucket to the gallon line with the faucet turned on full. Divide the number of seconds into 60 to determine the flow rate in gallons per minute. If the gallon bucket fills in 5 seconds, the flow rate is 60 ÷ 5, or 12 gallons per minute. If your water supply is a well, also note the reading on the pressure gauge for your pump as you do the test.

On a tracing paper overlay on your final plan, draw circles around parts of the garden that will be watered as a unit. The lawn might be one such unit. Ivy ground cover will need watering less often than a lawn, so it will be a different unit. Do not include areas where water will be applied to each plant instead of the whole planting—individual plants can be served by a drip system.

The parts catalog will show various kinds of sprinkler heads and specify the area each can cover. Select the sprinkler heads you need and trial-locate them in each watering unit on your overlay. Use a compass to draw an arc showing

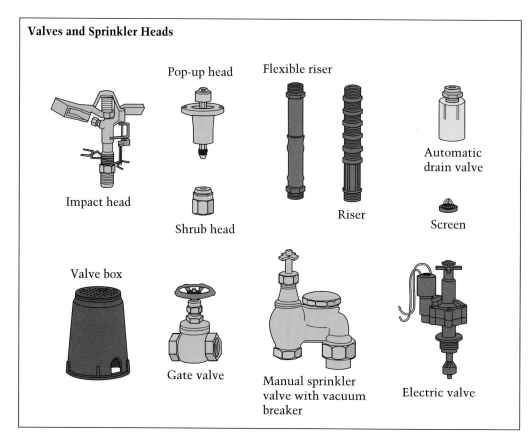

Valves and Sprinkler Heads

Pop-up head

Flexible riser

Impact head

Shrub head

Riser

Automatic drain valve

Screen

Valve box

Gate valve

Manual sprinkler valve with vacuum breaker

Electric valve

Irrigation Areas

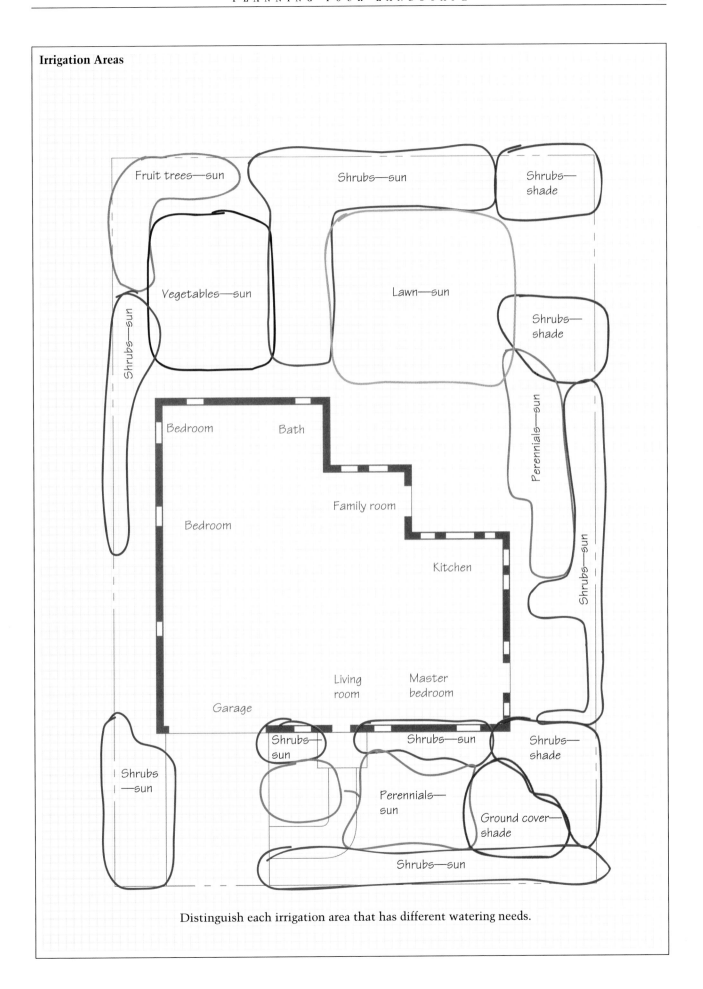

Distinguish each irrigation area that has different watering needs.

Head Location

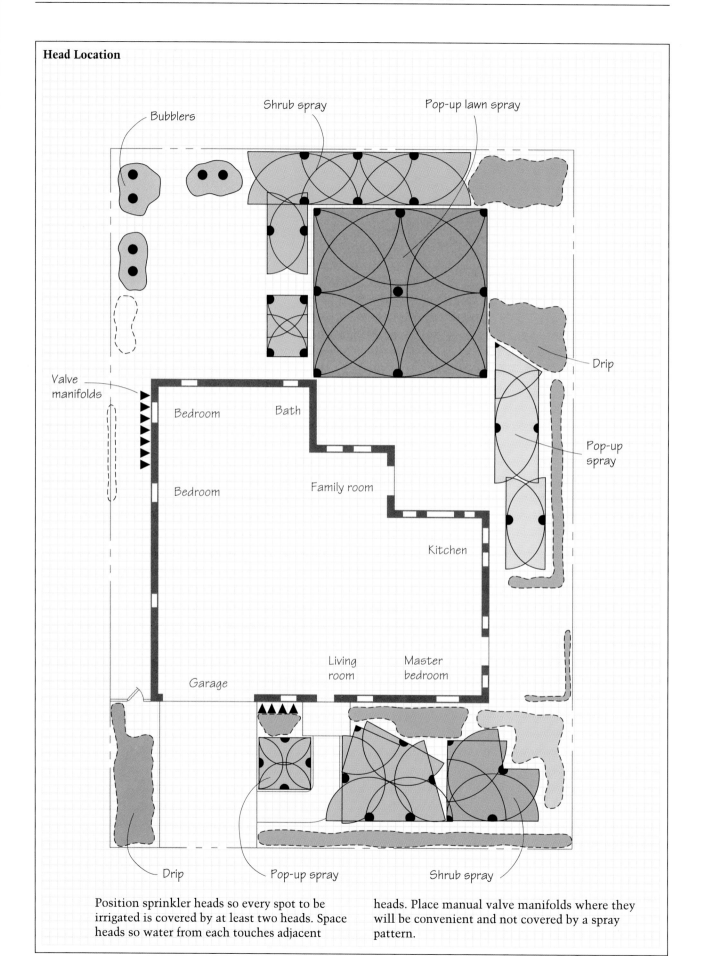

Position sprinkler heads so every spot to be irrigated is covered by at least two heads. Space heads so water from each touches adjacent heads. Place manual valve manifolds where they will be convenient and not covered by a spray pattern.

where each head will throw its water. Adjust the location of the heads so the water thrown by one head almost touches adjacent sprinkler heads. This will mean each part of the lawn is watered by at least two heads. The more evenly you can plan the water coverage, the more efficiently you will be able to water.

Now you need to establish circuits, or groups of heads that will be controlled by the valve. Write the flow rate (sometimes called precipitation rate in the catalogs) of each head next to it. Group the sprinkler heads into trial circuits and add up the flow rate in each. The total flow rate for each circuit should be no more than 80 percent of the flow rate of the hose bibb that supplies it.

Next place the manifold, the collection of valves that control the sprinkler system, on

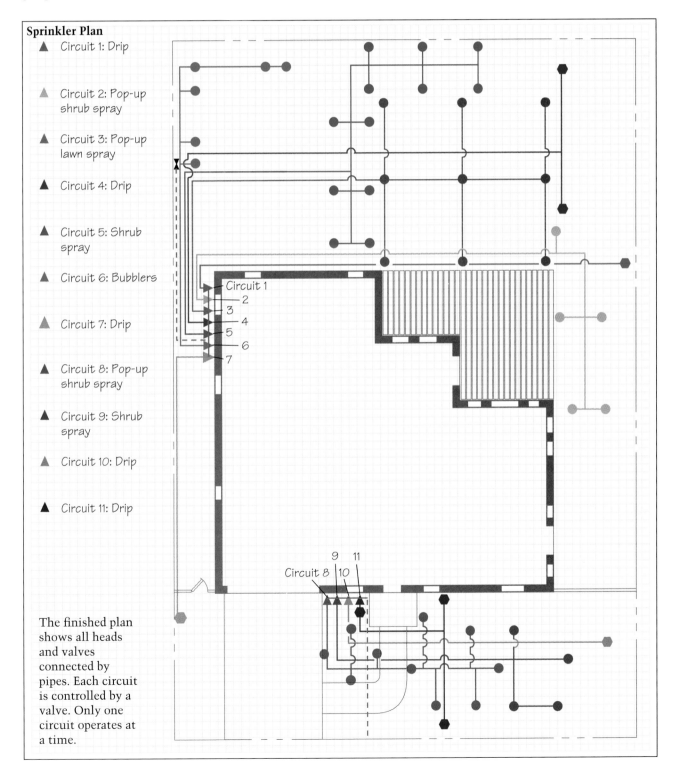

Sprinkler Plan

▲ Circuit 1: Drip

▲ Circuit 2: Pop-up shrub spray

▲ Circuit 3: Pop-up lawn spray

▲ Circuit 4: Drip

▲ Circuit 5: Shrub spray

▲ Circuit 6: Bubblers

▲ Circuit 7: Drip

▲ Circuit 8: Pop-up shrub spray

▲ Circuit 9: Shrub spray

▲ Circuit 10: Drip

▲ Circuit 11: Drip

The finished plan shows all heads and valves connected by pipes. Each circuit is controlled by a valve. Only one circuit operates at a time.

Pop-up lawn sprinkler heads lie flush with the ground when not in use, then rise a couple of inches when the water comes on, so the spray clears the grass. They are available in full-, half-, and quarter-circle spray patterns, as well as in a few other configurations for odd corners.

your plan. If you will have a manual system, choose a convenient place for the manifold—a place that is not watered by any of the sprinkler heads. If you will have automated valves operated by a timer, they can be placed wherever you wish.

If you will be using a timer (they are wonderful time-savers if you water regularly, and they will water your lawn while you're on vacation, too), place it near an outlet for electricity and as close to the valves as possible. Timers are often placed in garages.

Now plan the water lines. One line should connect the manifold to the water supply. Another should go from each valve to one circuit of sprinkler heads, carrying water to each head. Group the lines in common ditches wherever possible. Observe the guidelines about ditches in the section on hose systems (see page 43). If you use electric timers, their wires will also go in ditches, usually the same ones that carry the water pipes. On your plan, indicate all the ditches.

Designing a Drip System

Drip systems deliver water to the base of each plant, a drop at a time. Unlike sprinkler systems, which operate on household water pressure of 40 to 60 pounds per square inch, drip systems use 10 to 30 pounds per square inch. Because of the low pressure, lines and connections can be lighter and, therefore, easier to work with. Drip systems are intermediate in

cost between hose-end systems and sprinkler systems. When they are working well, they require no attention at all. They contain many parts that can come loose and small holes that plug up easily, however, so they must be monitored regularly.

Because parts are inexpensive and connections are easy to make and re-make, drip systems aren't usually planned in as much detail as sprinkler systems. At this point, all you need to consider is a water distribution point. This might be a hose bibb at the house. If your yard is very large, plan to install water lines to distant points. Select the parts you will need from a catalog. If your local irrigation dealer can't supply one, see page 92 for a supplier.

FINISHING THE PLANNING

By now, you know in some detail exactly what you want in your landscape. You know the structures you want to build, their dimensions, and the materials they will be made of. The irrigation system is designed, trees and shrubs selected, and flower beds and ground covers planned.

All this planning is documented in a final plan, overlays, and probably some detail plans. Only one more step remains in the planning process: making a cost estimate and schedule. These two documents summarize the cost of the landscape in dollars and time, and the process of creating the summary should help you use dollars and time efficiently. Making a cost estimate and schedule can help avoid unpleasant surprises and give you a feeling of being in control of the situation.

Making a Cost Estimate

You are now able to make a cost estimate that will be more accurate than one made when you first conceived of the project. You will make this estimate from a detailed shopping list.

Begin the list by "taking off"—putting into a list—each item on the final plan. Place a fresh piece of tracing paper over your final plan and, working in categories, check off every item as you list it. List each plant in as much detail as possible, including the size you will purchase, if you have decided that. When you list building materials, remember things like nails, hardware, and paint or stain. As you take items off the sprinkler system plan, count pipe fittings as well as heads, valves, and pipes.

Read through the final two chapters of this book to be sure that you have not overlooked anything.

To turn these shopping lists into a cost estimate, take the lists to a hardware store, lumberyard, or garden center, where an employee may help you estimate costs. Or locate each item yourself, note its cost, and add up the total.

Commercial contractors often add a "contingency" factor to compensate for overlooked items, changes in the plan, and unforeseen problems. This extra amount is a percentage of the total, up to 40 percent. Unless you are used to cost estimating, give yourself a contingency factor of 20 to 40 percent.

Making a Schedule

A schedule is another estimate, but of time rather than money. Schedules are most easily made in four steps: identifying tasks, sequencing the tasks, estimating the time each will take, and putting it all on a calendar.

The way you identify tasks depends on how you prefer to work. A "task" might be one weekend's work, or it might be a sequence of steps that ends with the yard relatively neat—a point at which you could halt for a while. Make a list of these tasks. Don't forget things like shopping for materials and cleaning a site before the start of construction. Sequence the tasks by listing them in order. You probably did this as you made the initial list, but if not, do it now.

Assign a duration, in hours, days, or weeks, to each task. Be realistic, allowing time to make mistakes and work out problems. Now fit the job to a calendar.

Up to this point, the entire job existed in a vacuum, as if it had the whole universe to itself. From here on, however, life begins to impinge on it. Take into account the season and probable weather as you plan. The best times to plant are spring and fall, in that order. However, planting can be done whenever the ground is not frozen or too wet to dig. Also remember your own personal and family schedules. Leave time for ordinary life—and don't forget about holidays, which can affect the availability of supplies and helpers.

A schedule, like a budget, is an estimate, and changes as the job progresses. Don't think of your schedule—or your budget—as fixed; see them as mutable entities that can adjust to circumstances.

Landscaping Tasks

These are some typical tasks leading up to a finished landscape. Your job will probably not have all the same tasks, and you may not do them in exactly this order, but this list will serve as a guide and checklist.

1. Measure the site and make a plot plan.
2. Plan the landscape.
3. Clean the site.
4. Shape the ground, making the rough grade.
5. Put in drainage and irrigation systems.
6. Build terracing and retaining walls.
7. Make patios and paths.
8. Build decks, fences, and other above-the-ground structures.
9. Make headers and raised beds.
10. Prepare the soil for plants, making the final grade.
11. Plant trees, shrubs, and hedges.
12. Plant flowers, vegetables, and ground covers.
13. Plant lawns.

This is a good time to evaluate the entire project. Can you afford the landscape you've planned? Are you willing to wait as long as you've planned for a finished landscape? The cost in money and the cost in time are dependent on one another, especially if you plan to finance the project from your living expenses, rather than withdraw from savings or borrow all the money for the project at once. The longer you take to finish the project, the longer you have to accumulate money. Also, scheduling the work over a long period allows you to carry out more money-saving steps, such as growing your own plants or searching for used building materials.

On the other hand, if you find the project costs less than you had thought it would, or if you come into an unexpected windfall, you can use the extra money to either speed up the project or upgrade the landscape. Perhaps you can install some of those expensive features you had deferred until later.

If you find that the budget and the schedule fit both your resources and expectations, you have finished the planning part of the job. The next step is to release the plan from the sterile confines of paper and pencil and send it into the real world of soil and plants.

Plants for Special Landscape Uses

Plants in these lists accomplish certain landscape tasks especially well. Each plant thrives in the climate zones shown next to its name. See the Plant Climate Zone Map on the opposite page to find out which zone you are in.

Ground Covers for Erosion Control

These plants have strong root systems that help stabilize soil on banks and slopes. Many are vines that trail on the ground, giving added soil protection.

Akebia quinata (Fiveleaf akebia) 4–9
Arctostaphylos uva-ursi (Bearberry) 2–9
Baccharis pilularis (Dwarf coyote brush) 7–10
Ceanothus griseus var. *horizontalis* (Carmel creeper) 7–10
Cistus spp. (Rockrose) 8–10
Coprosma × *kirkii* (Coprosma) 8–10
Coronilla varia (Crown vetch) 3–8
Cotoneaster spp. (Cotoneaster) 3–10
Gazania rigens var. *leucolaena* (Trailing gazania) 9, 10
Hedera helix (English ivy) 5–10
Hemerocallis spp. (Daylily) 3–10
Juniperus spp. (Juniper) 2–10
Lantana montevidensis (Trailing lantana) 8–10
Lonicera japonica 'Halliana' (Japanese honeysuckle) 4–10
Mahonia repens (Creeping mahonia) 5–10
Parthenocissus quinquefolia (Virginia creeper) 4–9
Phalaris arundinacea var. *picta* (Ribbongrass) 5–10
Polygonum cuspidatum var. *compactum* (Fleeceflower) 4–10
Pyracantha koidzumii 'Santa Cruz' (Santa Cruz firethorn) 6–10
Rosa wichuraiana (Memorial rose) 5–10
Rosmarinus officinalis 'Prostratus' (Dwarf rosemary) 8–10
Vinca spp. (Periwinkle) 5–10

Edible Ornamentals

These ornamental plants have edible parts. Some are known primarily as food plants, but they are attractive enough for a place in the landscape. Others are known primarily as ornamentals, but they are edible and tasty.

Ceratonia siliqua (Carob) 9, 10
Corylus avellana (Filbert) 4–8
Diospyros spp. (Persimmon) 5–10
Feijoa sellowiana (Pineapple guava) 9, 10
Vitus species (Grape) 4–9

- All common fruit trees have beautiful blossoms and can be pruned attractively. Citrus are excellent ornamentals.
- Most herbs are attractive in a flower border.
- Strawberry, especially the runnerless alpine strawberry
- Scarlet runner bean
- Carrots and chives are effective border plants.
- Ruby Swiss chard
- Most salad greens, including fancy lettuce and the chicories

Plants to Attract Hummingbirds

Many of these plants have red flowers with deep tubes that can be reached only by hummingbirds' long tongues.

Aquilegia canadensis (Columbine) 2–8
Buddleia davidii (Butterfly bush) 5–9
Campsis radicans (Trumpet vine) 4–9
Castilleja coccinea (Indian paintbrush) 3–9
Delphinium cardinale (Scarlet larkspur) 8, 9
Fuchsia spp. (Fuchsia) 5–10
Heuchera sanguinea (Coralbells) 5–10
Kniphofia uvaria (Red-hot-poker) 6–10
Lobelia cardinalis (Cardinal flower) 2–7
Lonicera japonica (Japanese honeysuckle) 3–9
Lonicera sempervirens (Trumpet honeysuckle) 3–9
Lupinus spp. (Lupine) 4–10
Mimulus cardinalis (Monkeyflower) 7–9
Monarda didyma (Beebalm) 4–7
Penstemon cardinalis (Beardtongue) 9, 10
Salvia splendens (Scarlet sage) 5–10
Tropaeolum majus (Nasturtium) All

Plants to Attract Butterflies

These nectar-rich flowers often face up and are surrounded by petals, allowing the butterfly to land and feed.

Achillea spp. (Yarrow) All
Asclepias tuberosa (Milkweed) 3–10
Aster spp. (Aster) 4–10
Astilbe spp. (Meadowsweet) 4–10
Buddleia davidii (Butterfly bush) 5–9
Centaurea cyanus (Bachelor's-button) All
Coreopsis spp. (Coreopsis) All
Cosmos spp. (Cosmos) All
Dahlia spp. (Dahlia) All
Echinacea purpurea (Purple coneflower) 3–10
Hemerocallis spp. (Daylily) 3–10
Lavandula spp. (Lavender) 8–10
Lonicera spp. (Honeysuckle) 3–9
Rudbeckia hirta (Black-eyed-susan) All
Solidago spp. (Goldenrod) 3–10
Syringa spp. (Lilac) 3–7
Wisteria spp. (Wisteria) 5–10

"Crack" Plants to Put Between Pavers

Use between stepping-stones or at the edges of paths. They all tolerate foot traffic, and many release fragrance when stepped on. These can also be used as a light-duty path.

Achillea tomentosa (Woolly yarrow) 3–10
Arenaria balearica (Corsican sandwort) 3–9
Chamaemelum nobile (Chamomile) 7–10
Duchesnea indica (Mock strawberry) 5–10
Fragaria chiloensis (Beach strawberry) 6–10
Glechoma hederacea (Ground ivy) 4–10
Laurentia fluviatilis (Bluestar creeper) 9, 10
Phyla nodiflora (Lippia) 9, 10
Sagina subulata (Irish moss) 4–10
Soleirolia soleirolii (Baby's-tears) 8–10
Thymus praecox arcticus (Creeping thyme) 3–10
Vinca minor (Common periwinkle) 5–10

Climate Zone Map

Approximate range of average annual
minimum temperature for each zone.

Zone 1	Below -50° F
Zone 2	-50° F to -40° F
Zone 3	-40° F to -30° F
Zone 4	-30° F to -20° F
Zone 5	-20° F to -10° F
Zone 6	-10° F to 0° F
Zone 7	0° F to 10° F
Zone 8	10° F to 20° F
Zone 9	20° F to 30° F
Zone 10	30° F to 40° F
Zone 11	Above 40° F

This climate zone map is based on the average low
temperatures for each zone. Use it as a starting point
for selecting plants that will thrive in your yard, but
recognize that local factors can affect the winter cold
in your area. For example, if you live near a large body
of water, your yard may support plants that are hardy a
zone or two south of your location. If you live at a high
elevation, you may be a zone or two colder than what is
shown on the map.

Based on the 1990 USDA Climate Zone Map

Building Your Garden's Basics

You've planned an economical landscape.
Now realize more savings by doing the major
construction work yourself.

At last you can get your hands dirty! It's time to begin moving soil around and building garden structures. Obviously, you'll be causing disruption in your yard. To keep it from lasting longer than necessary, plan your time so you can work quickly through the messy parts of the job. Arrange to fill in ditches and clean up during periods when you can't work steadily.

It's normal to deviate from your plans as the work progresses: Unforeseen obstacles arise or you change your mind about the best way to accomplish something. The working landscape plan shows your intentions at the beginning of the job, but probably won't be an accurate picture of the landscape when the job is finished. Keep records of changes by creating "as-built" plans of the landscape.

The changes that are especially important to record are those you can't see easily—the changes in underground work and the choice of plant species. Keep several separate as-built plans: one each of the underground parts of the drainage system, the irrigation system, and the actual plantings. Make these plans as if somebody else were going to be reading them—as somebody might. For instance, irrigation and drainage systems may need to be extended or repaired in future years, and a plan of where lines are actually laid and what is connected to what will save a great deal of digging and detective work then.

Keep as much information as possible about the woody and perennial plants you put in the ground. The record will be helpful in the future if you want to match a plant variety with an exact duplicate or just tell a friend who admires the fall color what variety a tree is.

When you install landscaping yourself, you'll want to do the construction in
stages. Built first, the deck in this yard is already in use. Now the lawn and its
retaining wall are being installed as a separate project.

high prices, you can sometimes find these materials in a wall or old building you can purchase and demolish yourself, or you may be able to salvage a pile of cobbles where a street was repaved.

Aggregate paving   Decomposed granite, shale, and other types of weathered rock are among the least expensive paving materials. If the rock is properly laid, it forms a surface that looks like packed earth, but it is weed-free and doesn't get muddy.

Gravel   Another inexpensive loose paving material is gravel. It needs no preparation other than an edging to contain it; you need only dump it on the site and spread it out. Its appearance and utility as a paving material depend on the gravel. Investigate it carefully before selecting (see page 38).

Broken sidewalk   This paving material is difficult to handle because of its weight and strength. It is usually free, however, and it can be one of the most satisfactory materials in the garden. Broken sidewalk can be used for paving and even to construct retaining walls, raised beds, and garden walls. Ask the city street department, or one of the contractors working on the streets, where sidewalks are being torn up. You will probably be able to haul it from the site at no cost.

These concrete pavers are made in an unusual shape that lends itself to interesting designs.

Brick   One of the most popular garden materials, brick is beautiful in almost any setting. Used brick is generally preferred for its soft, natural look. (Most "used" brick is new and "weathered" with splashes of color.) Bricks vary in their porosity. Hard bricks are fired at higher temperatures and are less porous than soft bricks. Soft, porous bricks readily absorb water, which freezes and expands in cold weather, cracking the brick. Therefore, in your landscape, use only hard, exterior-grade bricks.

Genuine used brick is in such demand that it often commands higher prices than new brick. But brick structures are plentiful enough in some areas that a little exploring will turn up inexpensive sources.

Brick pavers are made for patio and path paving. They are half the thickness of bricks.

Natural stone   In some parts of the country, you can have all the stone you want, free for the hauling. If you have to buy stone at a stone yard, it is expensive. For more information about working with natural stone, see one of the books listed on page 92.

Tile and concrete pavers   Tile is usually expensive, depending on its style. Be certain that the tile you choose is suitable for outdoor use. Unglazed tiles are subject to damage from moisture and freezing; some glazed tiles are extremely slippery when wet. Concrete pavers are quite inexpensive. You can make concrete pavers yourself fairly simply, but if you are going to go to that trouble, it might be easier just to pour a concrete patio.

Concrete   You can buy cement and aggregate and make your own concrete at a cost of about 50 cents per square foot. Mixing your own concrete isn't complicated, but it is hard work. Don't attempt to mix more than a couple of wheelbarrowsful of concrete by hand; rent a mixer instead. If you need more than a yard of concrete, purchase it ready-mixed. The convenience will more than offset the cost.

Concrete can often be pumped right into the form, saving you the difficult task of wheelbarrowing it from the curb. Of course, pumped concrete costs more than concrete delivered to the curb. For the greatest savings in small amounts (1 yard or less) of premixed concrete, haul it yourself in a special trailer you can rent from the ready-mixed concrete plant. It can be towed behind an ordinary car.

Buying Plants

You may already have arranged to grow or acquire many of your plants by starting seeds, by propagating from cuttings, or by placing an advance order with a nursery (see page 41).

For the remainder of your plants, explore your area for growers and wholesale nurseries. Often, wholesalers cannot give you the personal assistance you would get at a retail nursery, and they may not be willing to sell just a few plants. But if you need a large quantity of one type of plant, a wholesaler might have them for half their retail cost.

It pays to shop around for plants and to bargain a bit at the nurseries. Use the fact that you are landscaping an entire yard to ask for a discount. Ask how you can get price breaks—for instance, you might be able to realize savings by ordering well in advance or at certain times of the year. Nursery operators are happy to make business deals if you spend enough money to make it worth their time. As in any shopping, look for sales.

Arrange for the nursery to deliver the plants when you are ready for them. Many nurseries will assemble your order and care for the plants until you are ready to plant.

Renting Equipment

Tool rental agencies are very useful to builders, both amateur and commercial. Even commercial landscapers don't own all the equipment they use infrequently, such as large rotary tillers, weed mowers, tractors, power posthole diggers, and cement mixers. Visit the rental outlets in your area and see what tools are available. You might decide that renting a tool as simple as a wheelbarrow, for a few dollars a day, is more economical than purchasing it for 10 times the total rental fee.

Some of the most useful tools you rent will be the expensive gas- or electric-powered items. A small front-end loader or bulldozer will save many days of hard work. Rental agency personnel can give you valuable tips about using their equipment. If you're not sure how to accomplish a specific job, ask at a rental agency; it is likely to have a tool that will make the job simple.

PROTECTING TREES

Before doing any work, even cleaning up, protect the trees you intend to keep. If you will use heavy equipment around them, use wire or nylon cord to bind lengths of scrap or cheap lumber to the trunks. You can leave the protection in place for months, if need be, without harm to the trees.

Trees absorb most of their water from the top foot of the soil under their branches. Some roots extend deep into the soil to anchor the tree, but the topsoil immediately under it is a reservoir for water, nutrients, and oxygen. Adding more than a couple of inches of soil to the root area kills the roots by depriving them of air; lowering the grade under the tree may cut off or expose roots. Digging a ditch under a tree may also cut many roots. See page 77 for a technique that allows you to tunnel through soil with minimal damage to roots.

If you will be using a tool only briefly—this lawn roller is needed for just one afternoon—rent it instead of buying it. You can save money, even on low-cost items.

Top: The scrap lumber tied to this tree trunk has protected it from damage by construction equipment. Bark injuries may look minor, but because they can interfere with water flow to the top of the tree, they may damage it severely.

Bottom: If you need to lower the ground level around a tree, assure the tree's survival by leaving an area of unchanged grade under the tree. Support the soil with a retaining wall such as the one shown here, which has been made into an attractive bench.

If you wish to lower the grade around a tree, remove the soil that isn't being shaded by the tree, leaving the tree at a higher elevation than the surrounding ground. Build a retaining wall to hold the resulting bank in place, or taper the slope so it looks like a natural hill.

If you must fill around a tree, try building up only the ground outside the area it shades. This will leave the tree growing in a basin, which collects water and can drown the tree in wet weather. Nonetheless, if the basin can be drained or if the soil drains quickly, this method might be successful.

CLEANING THE SITE

Cleaning up might be a minor job or a major one, depending on the condition of your yard. If you are landscaping a newly built suburban house, it is probably surrounded by a desert of bare soil, scraped and packed by construction equipment. You will have little to clean up. But an old neglected garden might require removing trees, shrubs, old patios, and walks.

Begin by picking up anything loose and disposing of it. Large clean-up jobs may make it worthwhile to rent a trash receptacle from a disposal company—in urban areas, dump fees can be almost as expensive as the disposal company's charge.

Removing Plants

After loose material is removed, cut out weeds, brush, and unwanted garden plants and dispose of them. If there are many weeds, kill them before removal, as described on page 60. Depending on the size of the job, a rented tool might help. If the job is small, a handheld swing blade or weed scythe or a power weed-cutter might do the job best. If the job is large, rent a wheeled heavy-duty mower—such as a sickle-bar mower—that will cut through tough weed stems. Even heavier brush-removal equipment is available; ask the staff at the rental agency for advice about appropriate tools. To make digging out roots easier, leave a long stump on brush or small trees.

Where trees or shrubs will be planted more than a couple of feet apart, you can cut stumps off flush with the ground, because you will be able to avoid the stumps as you dig the holes. Some cut shrubs and trees resprout easily from the roots. If you don't take the time to kill or remove the roots, they will send out shoots with impressive vigor the following spring. Apply a brush-killer herbicide to keep such trees (see list below) from haunting you.

In some parts of the landscape—lawns, vegetable and flower beds, and most ground cover areas—the plants will be so close together that the easiest way to install them is to till the entire area. In these areas, you will need to dig out stumps and roots to allow tilling.

Because of their size, stumps of big trees pose special problems. Sometimes there is no alternative to the major task of digging them out. However, you might be able to avoid this effort by designing the stump into the garden as a stool, plant stand, or table support—it will last

for several years. Another option is to hire a tree contractor who will use special equipment to grind the stump below soil level. If you leave the roots in the ground, however, you are inviting termites, which might pose a danger to your house. Also, as the roots decay over the years, the ground will subside, leaving a depression that can cause serious damage to a structure above it, such as a patio. Ground settling won't be a problem in a flower bed, however.

To remove an old lawn, spray it with glyphosate herbicide, wait a week, then remove the turf. You can remove a very small lawn by cutting it into square-foot blocks with a sharp spade, then using the spade to slice the blocks loose, just under the turf. Rent a turf cutter to remove large lawns. Use the turf as a layer in

A turf cutter is a power tool that cuts the turf free from the soil so the turf can be rolled up.

Trees and Shrubs That Resprout From Roots

Eucalyptus
Poplars and cottonwoods (*Populus* spp.)
Privet (*Ligustrum*)
Silver maple (*Acer saccarinum*)
White alder (*Alnus rhombifolia*)
Willows (*Salix* spp.)
Most shrubs with multiple trunks coming
   from the ground, including poison ivy and
   poison oak

Making Compost

Composting is a sensible, beneficial way to dispose of plant material. You can compost any plant material smaller than the thickness of a finger. The simplest form of composting is to pile the cuttings in layers a few inches deep, in a pile at least 3 feet deep, wide, and high. Alternate layers of green and dry material if you have both. If all the material is dry, make a layer, then sprinkle it with nitrogen fertilizer or spread an inch of manure over it, then wet it thoroughly. Continue layering and wetting as the pile grows. If the plant matter is mostly green, mix it with some dry material, such as sawdust, and omit the fertilizer. Water the pile every month or so during dry weather. In a year, it will have rotted into a brown, crumbly compost that smells like the forest floor and improves any soil. If you are interested in making a more sophisticated compost more quickly, see the book list on page 92.

your compost pile (the glyphosate decomposes in soil or compost, so it won't contaminate the compost). Don't till the turf into the soil. This makes the soil difficult to work later, and raking the shredded turf out of the soil is more work than cutting it off the top.

Controlling Weeds

Removing weeds is simple, but keeping them out can be difficult. Keeping them out requires work now, as you install your landscape. The effort is worth it, though. Thorough weed control now will save hours of pulling weeds from ground covers and flower beds. The directions that follow apply to a landscape with lots of persistent weeds. If you have fewer weeds, modify the instructions.

Once removed, weeds can return from two sources: from roots left in the soil and from seeds. Roots are most easily killed before you remove the top of the plant; spray the foliage with a systemic herbicide, such as glyphosate. The tops need to be green and actively growing to absorb the herbicide. Wait a week for the herbicide to kill the roots, then remove the plant. Most roots won't resprout. If possible, spray the weeds during their growing season. Some deep-rooted weeds, such as couch grass and bindweed, will not be completely killed. They will resprout from surviving roots. Encourage their growth for a few weeks, then respray.

Seeds are more difficult to control than root growth. The best control method is to encourage seeds to germinate, then kill them before they can set another generation of seeds. Do this after you have finished moving soil and have reached the rough grade level (see "Shaping the Ground," opposite page). Water the ground and keep it damp to encourage weed seeds to germinate. In a few weeks, when the weeds are about 4 inches tall and before flowers form, kill them with an herbicide or hoe.

Repeat this procedure after the soil is prepared for planting, but before you plant. This time, to avoid bringing any more seeds to the surface to germinate, use an herbicide, not a hoe. In mild-winter regions where different weeds germinate in spring and fall, germinate and kill each set of weeds in its season. If the weed problem is especially severe, repeat this procedure until no more weeds germinate.

If you don't have time to wait for seeds to germinate, apply a preemergence herbicide after planting. The chemicals will remain in the soil for several weeks, killing any seeds that germinate. A few ornamentals are sensitive to certain herbicides; check the product label.

Moving Plants

Perennials, moderate-sized shrubs, and small trees can be moved to new locations. Try to move plants during their dormant season, or when they are quiescent—moving them successfully is difficult when they are actively growing. With any plant, move as much of the root system as you can and avoid breaking the ball of soil around the roots.

Begin by digging a hole in the new location. Follow the planting directions on page 85.

For perennials, with a sharp spade, dig around the roots on all sides. On the last cut, tip the spade back to lift the plant out of the ground. Carry the plant, on the spade, to its new location.

For shrubs and small trees too large to handle this way, cut back any low branches that are in the way, then dig a ditch 12 to 18 inches deep around the plant. Undercut the rootball from one side until it is almost ready to drop. Tuck a large square of burlap into the undercut, wadding half of it into the hole as far as possible. Now undercut from the other side until the rootball topples onto the burlap. Reach under the rootball, pull the burlap around it, and bind the burlap tightly around the rootball with string. Lift the plant onto a wheelbarrow or slide it onto a piece of plastic or plywood. Transport it to the new location, placing it in the hole with the burlap still in

Transplanting Large Shrubs

Prune lower branches

Dig a ditch around
the root ball

Cut under the root ball
on one side

Tuck burlap beneath
the root ball

Pull burlap under
the root ball

Root ball
wrapped in
burlap

Slide shrub to
new location on
sheet of plastic

place. Backfill the hole with soil halfway, then cut the string. Fold the burlap into the hole and finish backfilling. Finish planting according to the directions on page 85.

SHAPING THE GROUND

All the digging and soil moving happens at this stage of landscaping. You will solve drainage and erosion problems, tame steep slopes, and shape the landscape into the form called for in your plan (see page 33). When you are finished, the ground will be at the rough grade—within a couple of inches of the final level—and ready for paving and construction.

Moving Soil

Plan cuts and fills so you move soil as short a distance as possible. It's easier to push soil around with a rake than it is to throw it, and easier to throw it a few feet than load to it into a wheelbarrow and move it across the yard. The easiest way to change soil contours, and give them the most natural appearance, is by scraping. A small tractor (some are narrow enough to fit through a garden gate) equipped with a scraper blade in back and a bulldozer blade in front will scarify and loosen soil in the cut areas, then pull or push it along the ground to the fill areas and spread it evenly.

Topsoil is valuable. Subsoil must be improved for years before it supports healthy plant growth the way natural topsoil does. So save the topsoil when you move large amounts of soil. Scrape it off the work areas before you begin cuts and fills, stockpile it to one side, then spread it over both the cuts and the fills to finish the job.

Dig drainage ditches by hand or with a rented ditcher. For more information on digging ditches, see page 77.

Keep surface drainage in mind as you work. Avoid making low spots that will fill with water when it rains. If necessary, lay a spirit level on the soil to measure the pitch.

Building Retaining Walls

Retaining walls can be made in many ways, of brick, stone, wood, or concrete. The method described here is for stone or broken sidewalk, and it is applicable to walls up to 3 feet high. Walls higher than 3 feet hold back tons of weight and should be installed by a professional.

Begin by digging down to undisturbed earth, to create a base for the wall. Make the base as long as the wall is to be, and wide enough to accommodate the biggest pieces of building material. The base should tilt back 2 inches for every foot of its width. The earth that the wall will retain—the bank at its back—should be slanted back 2 inches for each vertical foot of the wall.

Terraces are a series of retaining walls on a hillside, with the soil cut to make one retaining wall used to fill behind the wall below it. If you are building terraces, fill the soil in as you build each wall. Compact soil as you go, to avoid settling and refilling later.

Laying Drain Lines

Begin digging ditches for drain lines in the same way you planned them, at the downstream end. So they can scour themselves clean and avoid plugging up with silt, drain lines need a slope of at least 1 foot for every 100 horizontal feet. Drain line is flexible, so the ditches don't need to be straight. Join connecting ditches at angles of 45 degrees or 90 degrees; fittings are made at these angles.

To maintain the minimum slope, use a tool called a ditching level. You can make one from an 8-foot length of 2 by 4. Drive a nail into the 4-inch-wide surface near one end, one inch from an edge. On the same face of the board, drive a second nail near the other end, 2 inches from the same edge. Tie a string between the nails, stretching it so it is taut. Hang a line level on the string. Check the slope of the ditch by putting the level on the dug surface, placing

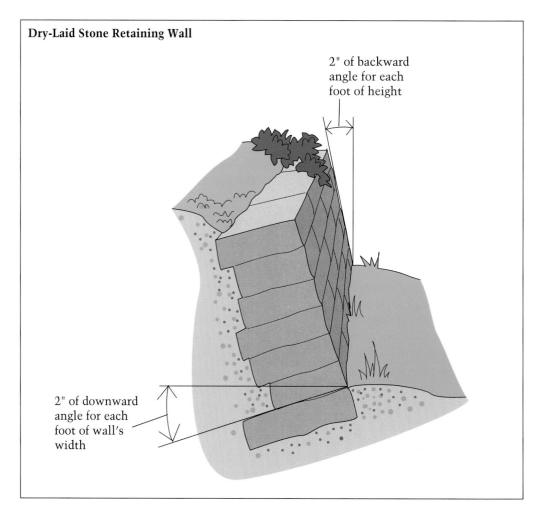

Dry-Laid Stone Retaining Wall

2" of backward angle for each foot of height

2" of downward angle for each foot of wall's width

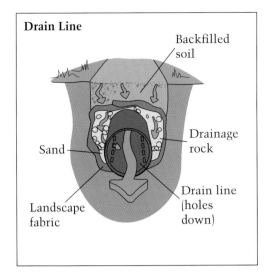

Drain Line

Backfilled soil

Drainage rock

Drain line (holes down)

Sand

Landscape fabric

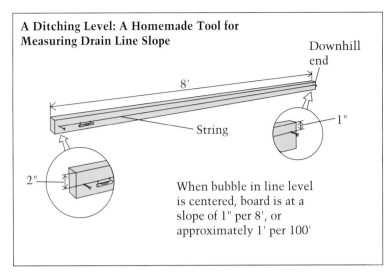

A Ditching Level: A Homemade Tool for Measuring Drain Line Slope

Downhill end

8'

String

1"

2"

When bubble in line level is centered, board is at a slope of 1" per 8', or approximately 1' per 100'

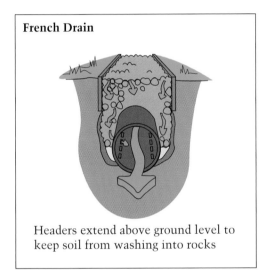

French Drain

Headers extend above ground level to keep soil from washing into rocks

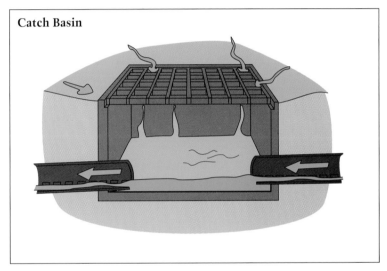

Catch Basin

on the downhill end the nail that is 1 inch from the edge. When the string is level, the 2 by 4 will be at a slope of 1 inch in 8 feet, which is about equal to a slope of 1 foot in 100 feet.

For an inconspicuous drain, line drainage ditches with porous landscape fabric. Cover the fabric with a 1-inch bed of sand. Lay the drain line on the sand, with the holes down, and cover it with several inches of drain rock. Fold the landscape fabric over the rock to envelop it. The fabric will filter out silt, keeping the drain rock from plugging up. Backfill the ditches.

If you don't mind a more conspicuous drain, install a French drain. It will provide faster drainage than the type covered with fabric cloth. Make the drain as the preceding paragraph describes, but backfill the ditch with drain rock right to the surface. The visible rock can be disguised as part of a gravel path, or let it be a decorative element beside a header

board or retaining wall. Place headers on both sides of the drain rock, at the surface, to keep soil from washing into it. For directions on installing headers, see page 83.

Catch basins can also be built into your underground drainage system. Like French drains, they collect surface runoff quickly and carry it to a drain line. Purchase a plastic or metal catch basin where you buy drain line.

Building Ponds

Modern flexible pool liners make ponds simple and inexpensive to build. These heavy fabric liners are made of flexible polyvinyl chloride (PVC) plastic, which can be molded to a pond of any shape.

Dig the pond in the shape you prefer, with a flat bottom from 20 to 26 inches deep and sides that slope back about 20 degrees from vertical. Cut an edging shelf 12 inches wide and 6 inches below water level all around. Cut another

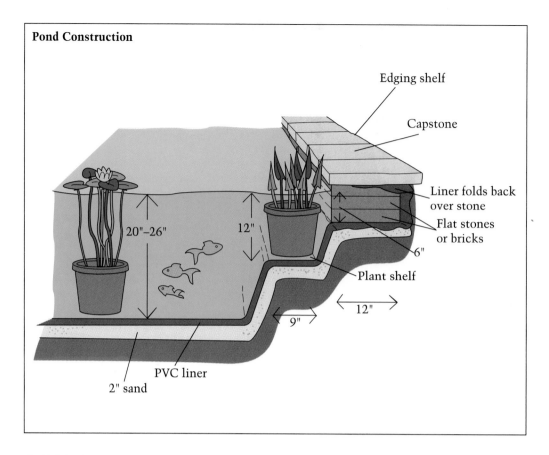

Pond Construction

Edging shelf

Capstone

Liner folds back over stone

Flat stones or bricks

Plant shelf

20"–26"

12"

6"

12"

9"

PVC liner

2" sand

shelf 6 inches deeper than the edging shelf and 9 inches wide around part or all of the edge. This second shelf will support aquatic plants in pots.

The length of the pool liner will be the length of the pond, including shelves, plus twice its depth, plus 2 feet. The width of the liner is calculated the same way—the pond width plus twice its depth, plus 2 feet.

Use a spirit level on a board to make sure the edging shelf is perfectly level all around. Smooth the soil in the hole and remove any rocks or roots that might tear the liner. To further cushion the liner, spread 2 inches of damp sand on the bottom and sides.

Spread the liner in the hole and use a hose to begin filling the pond with water. As it fills, arrange wrinkles in the liner sides into neat folds. Fill the pond to the top and check once more to be sure the edge is level.

Lay courses of flat stones or bricks on the edging shelf so the top stone is just above the surface of the water. Fold the liner back across the top of the stone; cut it at the middle of the stone. Finish the edge by adding a row of decorative stones or bricks, as capstones. Place the capstones on top of the liner and make sure each stone extends over the soil.

If your local garden center doesn't carry liners, pumps, pond plants, and fish, you can obtain them from one of the mail-order outlets listed on page 92. For more information about making and caring for ponds, see the book list on page 92.

PAVING

All paving is laid on a foundation of soil, and most requires some excavation so the paving surface remains at ground level. Most soils will support the light traffic of a path or patio, but if your soil is a clay that swells and shrinks enough to develop large cracks as it dries, excavate an extra 4 inches and fill that extra 4 inches with aggregate. This will stabilize the ground and prevent cracks or heaving in the paving as the ground changes due to moisture.

Installing Aggregate Surfaces

The simplest—and least expensive—patio and path surfaces are composed of aggregate. Some aggregates, such as decomposed granite or decomposed bluestone, become compacted in place. Other aggregate surfaces, such as gravel or decorative rock, remain loose. The main difference between the two types is the range of particle sizes. Gravel and decorative rock are composed of small rocks that are all about the same size. Aggregates that can be compacted contain a range of particle sizes, from pebble size down to "fines," or particles the size of dust. The fines fill in the spaces between the larger pieces, locking them together.

Begin building a compacted aggregate patio by excavating 4 to 6 inches of soil. If you wish, you can add an edging of wood, brick, or some other material (see "Laying Bricks in Sand," below, or the section on headers, page 83). The edging gives a neater appearance, but it isn't necessary.

Spread weed-block landscape fabric over the bottom of the excavation. This fabric has a weave tight enough to keep weeds from growing, but it allows air and water to pass through.

Cover the landscape fabric with 2 inches of aggregate, water it well, then compact it with a lawn roller while it's wet. Repeat spreading, watering, and rolling until the excavation is full. Leave a slight crown on the surface or create a slight slope from one side to the other, so water will run off quickly, without puddling.

A few weeds will start in the aggregate, but not very many, and those that start will be weak and easy to remove. Keep the aggregate clean. Contamination by garden soil will support vigorous weed growth.

To build a gravel patio, excavate as if you were building a patio of compacted aggregate. With gravel, an edging is important; it will keep the loose material from being kicked and scuffed out of the patio. Spread weed-block fabric on the bottom of the excavation, then fill the site to the top with gravel.

Laying Nonaggregate Paving

Some paving is laid dry on a bed of sand, and other materials are set in mortar on a concrete bed. Heavy, strong paving—such as broken sidewalk—is usually laid dry. Brick and cobblestones can be laid either dry or on concrete. Slate, flagstones, and tiles must be laid on concrete to keep them from breaking. As a general rule, set in concrete any paving material less than $1\frac{1}{2}$ inches thick.

Lay paving on as stable a base as possible. Undisturbed ground is best. When you dig, avoid disturbing the base soil; excavate only as deep as necessary. If the ground has been dug due to recent construction or gardening, dampen the soil, then compact it with a rented compactor or by pounding it with the end of a 4 by 4 timber.

In areas where the ground freezes, put a layer of base rock (pit-run gravel or crushed rock) under paving to keep it from heaving and becoming uneven as a result of repeated freezing and thawing. This layer should be 4 to 8 inches deep, depending on how cold the winters are. Spread 2 inches of damp sand on the base rock, compact it, and level it.

Wherever you plan to run irrigation pipes or wires under the pavement, place 2-inch or larger PVC pipe in the excavation before spreading the base rock. The pipe should be large enough to accommodate whatever pipes or wires will run under the paving, with room left over. Under long paths, place conduit every 50 feet, in case you want to put something under the path later. Extend the pipe beyond the edges of the walk or patio and plug the ends. Mark the locations of the ends on the landscape plan. Pipes and stiff wire can be pushed through the conduit. To put flexible wire, such as sprinkler system control wire, through the conduit, push a rod or pipe through from the further side, attach the wire to it, then pull the rod back through the conduit.

Paving With Broken Sidewalk

To lay a patio or path of broken sidewalk, dig an excavation the thickness of the sidewalk slabs plus 2 inches. Spread 2 inches of damp sand in the excavation, and set the slabs in place, leaving an inch or so between edges. Fill the spaces with topsoil and plant "crack plants" in them, leaving the surface of the soil in the cracks just lower than the surface of the concrete, so the soil won't be compacted by footsteps. See page 50 for a list of crack plants.

Laying Bricks in Sand

Like broken concrete, bricks, cobbles, and other thick pavers are laid in sand, but they need a rigid edging to prevent them from creeping. The edging can be 2 by 4 wood, benderboard, or metal headers (see page 83 for more information about headers). Brick set in concrete can also serve as edging.

If you're laying modular units, such as brick or tile, select a pattern (see following page). Try the pattern out on the ground and measure it carefully so you can build edgings just the right distance apart to contain the pattern.

Brick Patterns for Paths and Patios

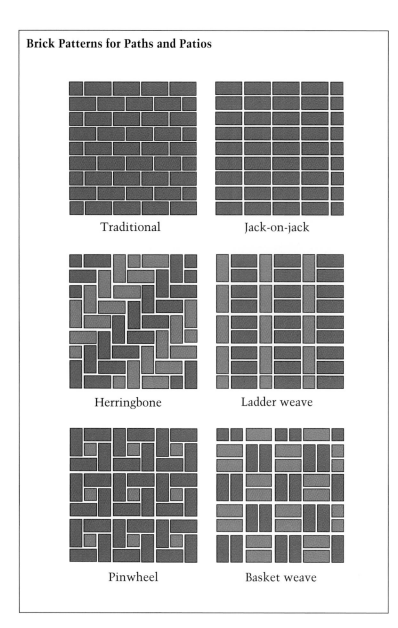

Traditional

Jack-on-jack

Herringbone

Ladder weave

Pinwheel

Basket weave

To save a great deal of work, select a pattern that doesn't call for too many cut bricks. If you buy the bricks from a masonry supply yard, the staff will cut some for you. If you have to cut them yourself, buy or rent a masonry chisel. Tap the chisel lightly with a masonry hammer to score a line around the brick. Lay the brick on a sand bed. With a sharp blow, break the brick at the score. Use the masonry hammer to chip off rough edges.

To make a brick patio with an edging of bricks in concrete, excavate as you would for a patio of broken sidewalk. Inside the excavated area dig a trench around the edges that is deep enough for the brick edging (the bricks can be set with any side up, depending on the appearance you wish)—plus another 8 inches—and 2 inches wider than the side of the brick that will be up. Be sure the edgings will be exactly the right distance apart, so the space between them can accommodate the pattern you have selected. Tamp 4 inches of base rock into the trench and pour 6 inches of concrete on top of it. (If you live in an area where the ground usually freezes, you will need more than 4 inches of base rock. For more information, read the next section, "Working With Concrete.") Press the edging bricks 2 inches into the concrete. Lay them so the edges are touching—you will not put mortar between them.

The next day, or after the concrete has hardened, make a screed similar to the one shown in the illustration below. Tamp 4 inches of base rock into the excavation and cover it

Dry-Laid Brick Patio

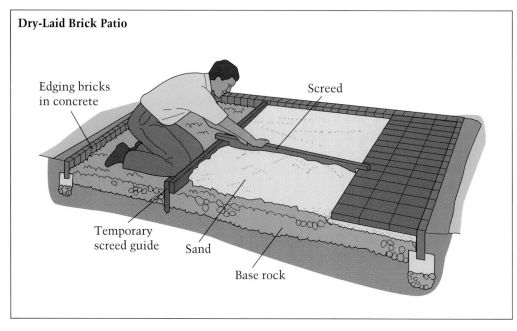

Edging bricks in concrete

Screed

Temporary screed guide

Sand

Base rock

with 2 inches of sand. Screed the sand level. If you are laying a patio that's too wide for a screed, make a temporary screed guide on which to rest one end of the screed.

To lay the patio bricks in the sand, work from nonexcavated surface, to avoid disturbing the sand. Lay the first row of bricks on the sand, with the edges touching. Do not trap sand from the base between them. Level the bricks by laying a board across several and tapping the board with a hammer. Place a sheet of plywood over these bricks and kneel on it to set the next row of bricks in place. Continue to the end, always working on plywood over the laid bricks.

After all the bricks are laid, sprinkle sand across them and sweep it into the cracks, where it will hold the bricks in place. (If the sand is damp, let it dry on the bricks before sweeping.) Repeat until the cracks are completely filled. After a few days or weeks, the sand will have settled. Sweep more into the cracks so they are full.

Working With Concrete

This versatile material can be finished in a variety of ways to create different effects from formal to rustic. As with other paving materials, you will pour the concrete on at least 4 inches of base rock—more if the ground freezes.

Where the ground freezes, reinforce the perimeter of a patio by digging a 6-inch-wide ditch around the edge to below the frost line. Half-fill the ditch with base rock. Place two

lengths of $3/8$-inch reinforcing rod (rebar) on the base rock, elevated 3 inches on small stones, so the rebar will be enclosed by concrete after it is poured.

To ensure straight edges for the patio, make forms from 2 by 4 lumber. If the forms need to be curved, use benderboard or strips of $1/4$-inch plywood or material such as Masonite hardboard. On the outside of the forms, place a wooden stake every 4 feet. Nail the forms to the stakes.

To keep water from puddling on the patio or the path during rainstorms, make the forms a little higher on one side than on the other. The finished patio or walk should have a pitch of $1/8$ inch per foot.

Because temperature changes cause concrete to contract and expand, it should not be poured in large single slabs. Plan expansion joints at least every 10 feet along a path or every 10 to 15 feet on a patio. An expansion joint is softer than concrete. It is embedded in the concrete to keep it from buckling when the concrete expands in warm weather. Expansion joints can be permanent redwood 2 by 4s built as part of the form. In areas that freeze, nail 16-penny (16d) nails halfway through the 2 by 4s every foot or so. This will give the concrete a good grip on the wood and prevent the joint from heaving out of the patio.

If you prefer narrower joints, purchase asphalt-impregnated expansion strips made for this purpose. Place a 2 by 4 where you want the expansion joint, and place the expansion strip against one side of the lumber. Pour

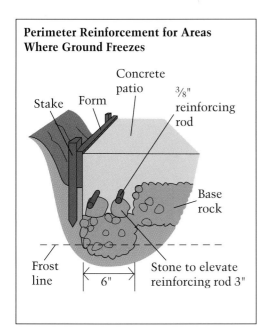

Perimeter Reinforcement for Areas Where Ground Freezes

Stake

Form

Concrete patio

$3/8$" reinforcing rod

Base rock

Frost line

6"

Stone to elevate reinforcing rod 3"

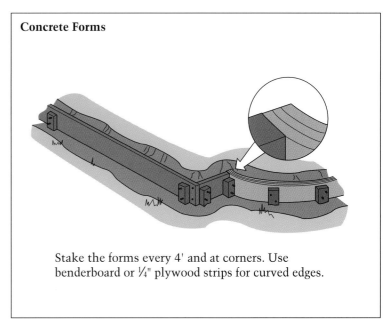

Concrete Forms

Stake the forms every 4' and at corners. Use benderboard or $1/4$" plywood strips for curved edges.

concrete on the side with the expansion strip first, then pour the other side. Carefully remove the 2 by 4, leaving the strip in place. The concrete will fill the space where the 2 by 4 was. Screed the concrete level, as described below.

You will need a cubic yard of concrete for every 80 square feet of a 4-inch-thick slab, plus an extra 10 percent for wastage. If you are mixing your own, purchase a yard of aggregate—mixed sand and gravel—and six sacks of Portland cement for every yard of concrete you need. Unless you are making only a small amount, rent a portable mixer. Start the mixer and measure the cement and aggregate into the mixer or a wheelbarrow by the shovelful: 1 shovelful of cement to 5 shovelfuls of aggregate. Add water slowly, until the concrete is just wet enough to flow. Be careful as you add water; it's easy to put in too much. If the mix becomes too wet, it will be weak; add more cement and aggregate (in the 1 to 5 ratio) until it is just right.

If you purchase ready-mixed concrete, have everything ready when the truck arrives, and several friends on hand with wheelbarrows to help you unload. If unloading takes more than 5 minutes per cubic yard, the concrete supplier will probably charge you for waiting time.

As you fill the forms, strike off the concrete—level it with a board laid across the forms. Use a sawing motion, working toward the unfilled part.

After the forms are filled and the concrete has lost its watery sheen, smooth the surface

Finishing Concrete

Striking off

Smoothing with bull float

Finishing

Edging

Top: Cut contraction joints at regular intervals in concrete. If the concrete should contract enough to break, it will break along these grooves, where the cracks will be invisible. Bottom: All four quarters of this patio plus the "brick" separating them are concrete. Two quarters are finished in exposed aggregate. The other two, and the separating bands, are stamped and colored to look like stone and brick pavers.

with a bull float or a darby, then finish it with a smaller wood float (see illustration on opposite page and explanation below). In about 45 minutes, after the concrete has begun to set up, slide an edging tool along the forms to round the slab edge and make it less likely to chip.

Every 10 feet, cut contraction joints across the entire expanse of concrete. A contraction joint is a line scored in the concrete along which the concrete can break if there is enough contraction to cause breakage. Expansion joints also allow contraction, so they function as contraction joints also. On a path, cut contraction joints at intervals of 1½ times its width. Cut the joints with a grooving trowel, using a board as a straightedge.

The final appearance of the concrete depends on the finishing technique you select. A wood float leaves a moderately smooth finish, the one most frequently encountered on paths. A smoother finish can be obtained with a steel finishing trowel, but such a finish is slippery in wet weather and not recommended for outdoor surfaces. For a rougher surface, pattern the concrete with a soft push broom or use leaves, cans, wooden letters, or other items you find around the house. Concrete can also be patterned with a stamping tool. These tools, which have patterns of cobblestones, bricks, flagstones, and other paving surfaces, can be rented; get directions for using them where you rent them. Concrete can also be colored.

Additives can be mixed into the wet concrete or worked into the surface after it is fin-

ished. One of the most attractive is called exposed aggregate. For the nicest appearance, buy river gravel in a color you like. As soon as the concrete is poured, sprinkle the gravel in a dense layer across the concrete. Work it into the concrete with a float, so the stones are just barely covered.

Let the concrete cure until you can just leave a fingerprint and you can walk gently on the surface. (Curing to this stage will take about 3 to 5 hours after the concrete is poured.) Then expose the surface of the pebbles by sweeping the concrete off them and washing it away. A couple of hours later, wash the pebbles once more to clean away any film of cement. A week or two later, wash the concrete with a mixture of 1 part liquid swimming pool acid to 4 parts water.

Finishing concrete, especially exposed aggregate, takes some skill. Judging the curing of the concrete is critical to achieving the effect you want. To gain experience, practice with a set of stepping-stones made of ready-mixed concrete poured into wooden forms. One sack will make four stepping-stones 1 foot square and 2 inches thick.

Concrete takes a month to cure completely. Keep it from drying out during this time by covering it with polyethylene film. Spread the film across it after the concrete has hardened enough so the plastic won't stick to it. Overlap seams generously, and weight down the edges with boards or soil. If covering the concrete is

difficult, sprinkle it with water several times a day during dry weather.

Laying Paving on Concrete

Thin paving, such as slate, *must* be laid on concrete to prevent breakage. Most other paving, including brick, will be more substantial and longer-lasting on concrete than other base materials. Excavate deep enough to accommodate 4 inches of base rock (where the ground freezes, go deeper if necessary, to go below the frost line), 4 inches of concrete, ¾ inch of mortar, and the paver. Spread and tamp down the base layer, then pour 4 inches of concrete on it. After the concrete has set, spread ¾ inch of mortar on a few square feet of concrete and set the pavers in it, leaving ⅜-inch gaps between them for mortar (space the pavers with a piece of ⅜-inch plywood). Continue spreading mortar and laying pavers, not spreading more mortar than you can cover with pavers in about 10 minutes.

After the mortar has set, fill with dry mortar the spaces between the pavers. Sweep mortar into the cracks, then wet the mortar with a fine spray from a hose. If the mortar settles below the surface of the pavers, fill the spaces again and spray again. When the mortar has set up enough to hold a fingerprint, use an edging tool to press the mortar into the spaces. Different edging tools will produce different effects.

As soon as you have tooled the joints, brush any mortar crumbs off the pavers. Clean any remaining mortar off the bricks, using a sponge

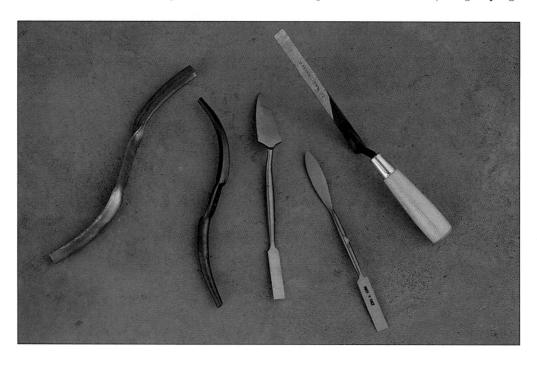

Edging tools are used to finish the mortar in brick joints. Each produces a different effect.

or piece of coarse cloth soaked in water. If the mortar is stubborn, clean the bricks with trisodium phosphate (TSP), available in paint and hardware stores. Any mortar that dries on the brick will be difficult to remove.

BUILDING A DECK

Decks can be very simple or quite complex. The one presented here is a simple design that can easily be modified to fit many situations. It is not attached to the house, so it can be used in any location in the yard. If the deck will be more than 2½ feet above ground level, add a railing. If it will be against the house, make the deck the same level as the house floor and leave a ½-inch space between the deck and the house. Be sure to obtain proper permits before building.

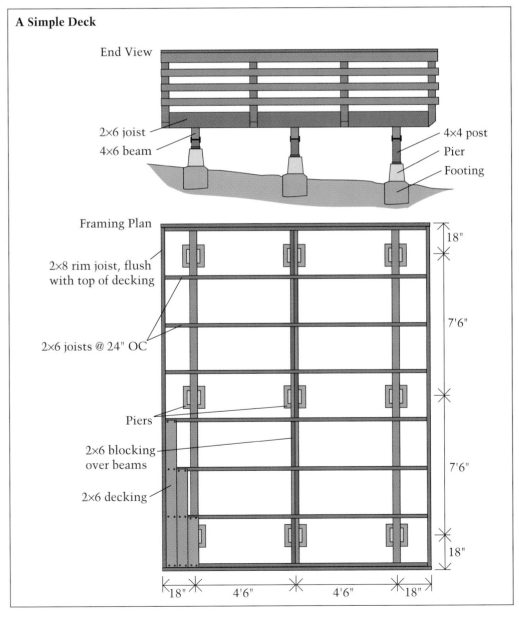

A Simple Deck

End View

2×6 joist
4×6 beam

4×4 post
Pier
Footing

Framing Plan

2×8 rim joist, flush with top of decking

2×6 joists @ 24" OC

Piers

2×6 blocking over beams

2×6 decking

18"

7'6"

7'6"

18"

18"   4'6"   4'6"   18"

Begin deck construction by locating the corners. Drive stakes into the approximate spots, then measure the two diagonals. If the diagonals are the same length and parallel sides are the same length, the corners are all square and the shape you have marked out is a perfect rectangle.

The directions that follow will guide you through all the basic steps in constructing a deck. If your design is more complicated, you will need to employ additional techniques. Detailed information on deck construction, as well as other deck plans, may be found in the books listed on page 92.

Laying the Foundation

To place the footings of the deck, construct batterboards and tie string, then use a line level and plumb bob to identify the positions of the three beams and one end of the deck as shown in the illustration below. Use a framing square to get the lines approximately square. After all the lines are in place, measure the diagonals and adjust the lines until the diagonals are equal.

Holes for footings should be 12 inches square. Dig to below the frost line (in areas where the ground doesn't freeze, dig the holes 12 inches deep). The bottom of the hole should be in undisturbed soil. Unless your deck is very large, buy ready-to-mix cement in bags and mix it in a wheelbarrow. Fill each hole with concrete and set a precast concrete pier in it, working the pier ½ inch into the concrete. Level the pier.

Set posts on each pier, with temporary braces to hold them plumb. Toenail each post to the nailing block on top of its pier; use 2 nails on each side. As shown in the illustration below, mark the posts at the right height for cutting, using a line level. Cut all the posts at the marks.

Installing Framing and Decking

Use post caps to attach the beams to the tops of the posts. Then toenail the joists to the beams. Install blocking over the center beam. Nail the rim joists over the ends of the joists, so their tops will be level with the decking. Attach the rim joists the same day as you install the joists, to prevent the joists from warping.

If the deck is against the house, begin laying the decking on the side by the house. To let

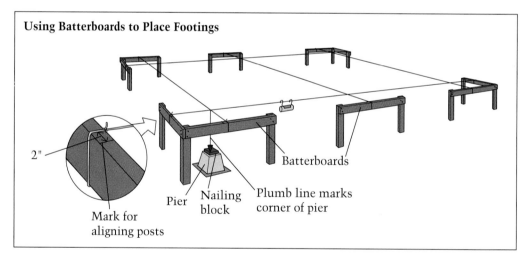

Using Batterboards to Place Footings

2"

Batterboards

Pier   Nailing block   Plumb line marks corner of pier

Mark for aligning posts

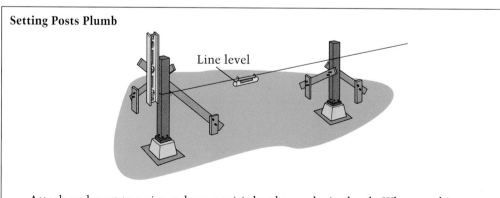

Setting Posts Plumb

Line level

Attach each post to a pier and use a spirit level to make it plumb. When marking the posts for cutting, allow ⅛" slope per foot in one direction for drainage.

water drain, leave a ½-inch gap between the deck and the house. Lay the decking so ends will butt at the center of a joist, but ensure that adjacent joints do not lie on the same joist. Lay each board so the end grain is convex—that is, the part of the board that used to be toward the outside of the tree should face up. Use 16d galvanized screw nails. Drive the nails at alternating angles, with 3 nails at each board end and 2 nails where boards cross a joist. To avoid splitting the boards, drill pilot holes for nails. Let all the board ends protrude over the edge.

Nailing and Cutting Decking

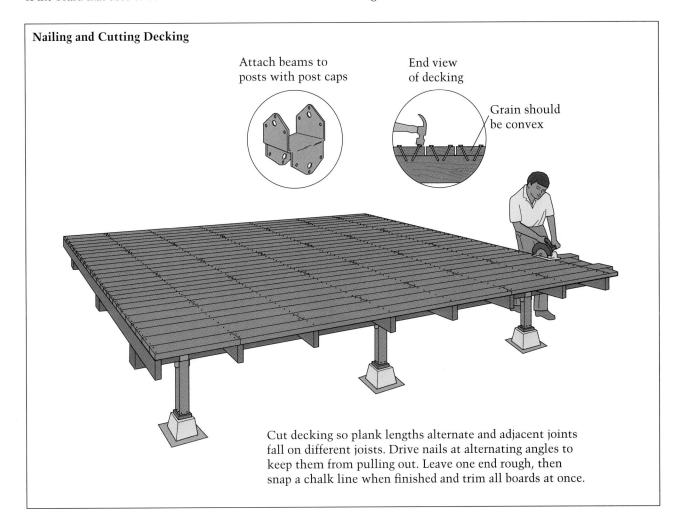

Attach beams to posts with post caps

End view of decking

Grain should be convex

Cut decking so plank lengths alternate and adjacent joints fall on different joists. Drive nails at alternating angles to keep them from pulling out. Leave one end rough, then snap a chalk line when finished and trim all boards at once.

Railings

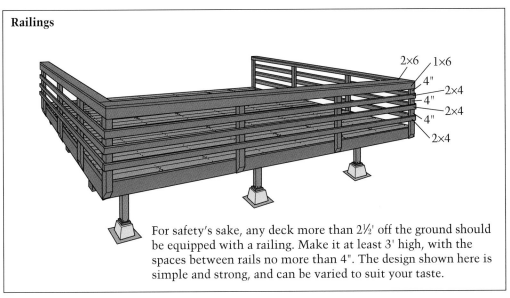

2×6   1×6
4"
2×4
4"
2×4
4"
2×4

For safety's sake, any deck more than 2½' off the ground should be equipped with a railing. Make it at least 3' high, with the spaces between rails no more than 4". The design shown here is simple and strong, and can be varied to suit your taste.

Steps

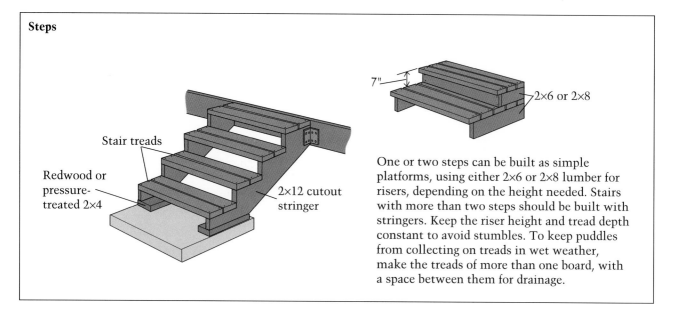

Stair treads

Redwood or pressure-treated 2×4

2×12 cutout stringer

7"

2×6 or 2×8

One or two steps can be built as simple platforms, using either 2×6 or 2×8 lumber for risers, depending on the height needed. Stairs with more than two steps should be built with stringers. Keep the riser height and tread depth constant to avoid stumbles. To keep puddles from collecting on treads in wet weather, make the treads of more than one board, with a space between them for drainage.

Every couple of boards, measure the distance from both ends of the board to the deck edge, to be sure the boards are parallel. You will probably have to make small adjustments. When all the boards are laid, snap a chalk line across the end and saw them all off at once.

The illustrations on page 73 and above will aid you in constructing railings and steps, if your deck requires them.

BUILDING FENCES

Fences may be screens for privacy and security, or they may be decorative elements to delineate spaces and guide traffic. The fence described here is a basic 6-foot, solid-board version that can be altered in many ways. For instance, just by changing the material, size, and spacing of the boards, it can become a 3-foot picket fence. For more detailed information about building fences, as well as other fence designs, consult the list of books on page 92.

Setting Posts

Lay out the fence by using batterboards and string (see illustration, page 72). With stakes, mark locations for end posts and corner posts, and for line posts. (Line posts should be no more than 8 feet apart.) Mark the batterboards 2 inches to one side of the string, and remove the string.

Postholes must be dug with a special tool—a shovel won't dig a hole deep enough. For most soils, you will need a clamshell digger, but augers and other types (including gas-powered diggers) work well if the soil is free of rocks.

You will probably also need a crowbar to loosen the soil. Dig holes for line posts 2½ feet deep and 12 inches in diameter, centered on the point marked by the stake. Dig holes for end posts and gateposts 3½ feet deep and 12 inches in diameter. Put 6 inches of drain rock in each hole.

After the holes are all dug, run a marking string on the marks that are 2 inches to the side of the centerline of each fence line. Drive a 16d nail 1 inch into the bottom of each post (this will keep the bottom of the post from shifting when you shovel in drain rock). Set a post in each hole, lining the posts up on the strings. Hold the posts in place with temporary braces. Place another 2 inches of drain rock around the base of each post.

Make up about one bag of ready-to-mix concrete for each hole. As you fill the hole, poke the concrete with a pipe or broomstick to release any air bubbles. Overfill it slightly and crown off the concrete with a trowel so water will run away from the post. Let the concrete set up overnight or longer before completing the fence.

Installing Stringers and Boards

Remove the temporary braces on the posts. Drive a nail in an end post, at the height the post should be. Attach a chalk line to it, measure the same height on the post at the other end of this line, pull the chalk line tight, and snap it to mark the top height on all the posts. Check the posts to make sure all were marked. Saw the posts off at the line. Repeat for any other fence lines.

Building a Fence

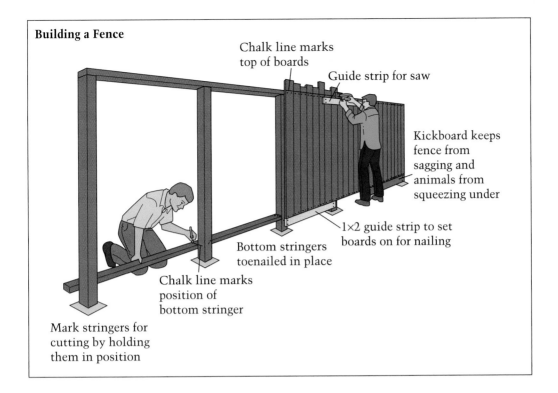

Chalk line marks top of boards

Guide strip for saw

Kickboard keeps fence from sagging and animals from squeezing under

1×2 guide strip to set boards on for nailing

Bottom stringers toenailed in place

Chalk line marks position of bottom stringer

Mark stringers for cutting by holding them in position

Nail the top stringer on top of the posts. Snap a chalk line to mark the height for the bottom stringers. The bottom stringers should be toenailed into place; drill angled pilot holes through the stringers to make toenailing easier.

On the side of the fence where you will attach the boards, nail a temporary guide between two posts, to mark the future level of the bottoms of the boards. Set one board at a time on the guide and nail the board into place. Every few boards, check with a level to be sure they are remaining plumb; make corrections if necessary. Move the guide as you work.

When all the boards are in place, snap a chalk line to mark the top edge of the boards. Nail a guide strip below the chalk line to serve as a rest for the edge of the shoe of your power saw. Cut the boards. Horizontal filler boards (kickboards) under the bottom stringers will prevent the fence from sagging and prevent animals from squeezing under the fence.

Installing Gates

Because gates move—and slam—they are subject to much more strain than fences. Select heavy-duty hardware and mount it firmly, using the largest and longest screws possible. To be sure everything will fit, purchase the hardware before laying out the gate. You will need hinges and a latch, and you may want a spring to close the gate automatically.

Gate Stop

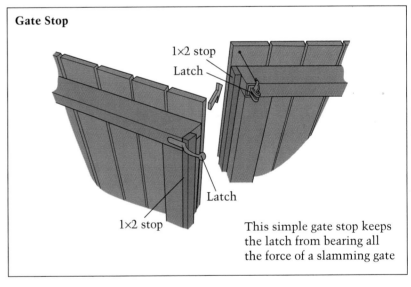

1×2 stop

Latch

Latch

1×2 stop

This simple gate stop keeps the latch from bearing all the force of a slamming gate

Measure the opening at top and bottom. Plan the gate to be about ¾ inch narrower than the opening; the exact size depends on your hardware. Cut the posts and rails. Working on a flat surface, nail the frame together. Adjust it to be square, then cut and nail the diagonal brace.

As you nail the boards, be sure to keep them square to the frame. Turn the gate over and attach the hinges. Place boards in the gate opening to raise the gate to the proper height; resting the gate on the boards, mark the posts for the hinge screws. Attach one screw for each hinge, and test the gate to be sure it clears. Set the rest of the screws and attach the latch.

INSTALLING IRRIGATION SYSTEMS

If you are putting in both drip and sprinkler irrigation systems, dig all the ditches, build any manifolds that will be shared by different systems, and lay all the pipes at once; do not put in one system at a time.

Although several materials are used in making plumbing pipe and connections, polyvinyl chloride (PVC) is the best for irrigation systems. It is inexpensive and easy to work with, requiring no investment in specialized tools and no special skills. It is available in a wide variety of sizes and wall thicknesses, but for almost all home irrigation systems, you will need only one size and two wall thicknesses.

Plumbing that will be under constant pressure—the pipes that run from the house to the valves—should be of iron pipe or Schedule 40 PVC—PVC pipe with a fairly thick and rigid wall.

Pipes downstream of the valves never have to bear full pressure. They can be of a gauge called Class 200. Class 200 is thick enough to resist a shovel, so you won't cut through a buried irrigation line without knowing it, but it is thin enough to be fairly flexible and easy to work with. To make connections with Class 200 pipes, you will use slip joints glued with PVC solvent.

Sprinkler heads are always manufactured to accommodate ½-inch connections, but over long runs ½-inch pipe will restrict water flow. Therefore, use ¾-inch pipe for the entire system, using adapters at each sprinkler head to attach the head. The price difference between ¾-inch and ½-inch pipe is insignificant, and you will appreciate the simplicity of using only one size throughout.

Two situations might call for deviation from these sizes and gauges. One involves a pipe downstream of the valves that is exposed to particular danger of damage. For example, if you couldn't bury a pipe below shovel depth because of shallow soil, it would be exposed to the risk of cutting with a spade or tiller. In such a case, use Schedule 40 PVC or iron pipe. You can also lay a piece of rot-resistant wood over the pipe for protection.

Parts of a Sprinkler System

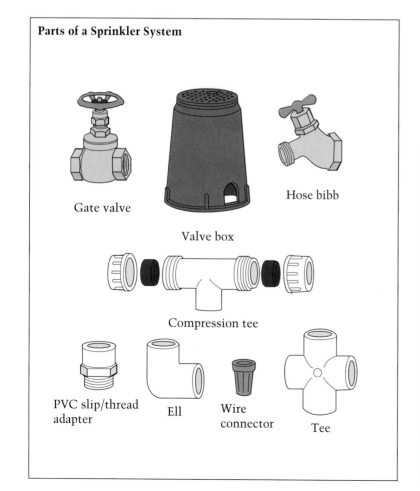

Gate valve

Valve box

Hose bibb

Compression tee

PVC slip/thread adapter

Ell

Wire connector

Tee

Working With PVC

Class-rated PVC is joined with smooth joints called slip joints, which are glued together with PVC cement. Cut the PVC to length with a PVC cutter or a hacksaw. Remove any burrs with a knife. Apply PVC primer to the surfaces to be cemented.

Using the dauber in the can, paint the male end of the joint with cement. Slip the pieces of the joint together and rotate one piece one-quarter turn to spread the cement in the joint. Wipe off any excess cement—the cement is a solvent and will weaken the joint if left.

Let the joint sit for several hours, according to the instructions on the cement can, before turning on the water.

The other situation that calls for deviation involves low household water pressure or flow rate. If you wish to hold down the number of circuits, you can economize on the available pressure by cutting into the water line, as close as possible to the water meter, and running 1- or 1¼-inch pipe to the valves. This reduces the pressure loss that is due to friction in the run to the valve. The result is more pressure and flow for the sprinkler heads.

Digging Ditches

Irrigation lines should be deep enough to be safe from any digging or tilling that might take place above them. Most tilling is 6 to 8 inches deep, and lawn aerators poke holes about 3 inches deep. Ditches under lawns should be at least 8 inches below the surface, and those under other parts of the garden should be 12 inches below the surface.

Use stakes to mark the locations of sprinkler heads and valves. Where ditches are to be dug, draw lines with agricultural lime, dribbling the lime from your hand or a tin can or through a large funnel.

If you are digging more than 50 feet of ditch, rent a power ditcher or trencher to save your back. These power tools work quickly and neatly. They are difficult to maneuver in tight spaces, however, and don't work well on hillsides. If you are digging by hand, a ditching spade—which you can also rent—will speed up the job.

Putting Pipe Under Sidewalks and Trees

Use iron pipe (the same diameter as the PVC irrigation line) to punch under existing walks and through tree roots. Attach a coupling to one end, and insert a plug into the coupling. Dig the irrigation ditches on both sides of the sidewalk or tree. If a ditch isn't at a right angle to the sidewalk or tree, dig a temporary ditch at a right angle to it. The temporary ditch should be long enough to lay the iron pipe in, plus another few feet. This ditch should be about 3 inches deeper than you want the irrigation line to be. Dig a small hole for the end of the iron pipe, at the place and depth you want to put the irrigation line. Place the plugged end of the pipe in the hole, and drive it through the ground with a sledgehammer. Every few blows, use a pipe wrench to turn the pipe one-quarter turn; this will keep it going straight. When the pipe reaches the ditch on the other side of the obstacle, remove the coupling and pull the pipe out of the hole. If necessary, clamp a vise grip or large pipe wrench to it and pry on the vise grip or wrench with a crowbar to remove it. Fill in the temporary ditch.

Plug
Pipe
Coupling

To avoid breaking up a sidewalk or cutting tree roots, make a hole by driving a homemade punch under the obstacle

To mark ditches, draw lines with agricultural lime. Dribble it from your hand or a trowel, or snip a corner from a small bag of lime and pour directly from the bag.

Adding Hose Bibbs

This is the time to install additional hose bibbs. Turn off the house water at the main shutoff or the water meter, and cut into the water line. You can branch off at the spot where the main line enters the house or at any convenient hose bibb. If you are connecting to a hose bibb on galvanized iron pipe, disassemble the valve and riser and reassemble them with a tee connection in the riser. If you are cutting into copper or PVC, or into iron pipe away from a hose bibb, cut out a section of pipe and install a compression tee. Because it simply clamps onto a pipe, a compression tee can serve as an attachment site anyplace in any type of pipe.

Attach ¾-inch Schedule 40 PVC or iron pipe to the tee and lay out the pipe and connections beside their ditches. If you are using iron pipe, rent pipe cutting and threading tools; staff at the rental agency will show you how to use them.

Assemble the pipe and connections in order, beginning at the connection to the existing system. Place a strip of pipe joint tape around each male thread before connecting it to the next piece. The tape will lubricate the joint and seat it more firmly.

The riser for the new hose bibb should be firmly attached to something. If it is not against a house wall or fence post, sink a 4 by 4 redwood post to mount it on. See page 74 for directions for sinking posts. Attach the riser to the wall or post with at least two plumber's straps held in place with screws rather than nails. Attach the hose bibb. Mount a hose reel next to the bibb and attach a hose to the bibb and reel. Build a small shelf or box—or mount a mailbox—to hold any hose-end attachments you will use with the hose. If the bibb is at the back of a flower bed or border, install a couple of large stepping-stones so the bibb will be easy to reach, and don't let shrubs grow in front of it.

Sprinkler Systems

Cut into the household water line close to the water meter. If the meter is buried near the curb, dig down to the line a few feet away from the meter, turn off the valve at the meter, and cut into the line. Fit the line with a compression tee and a gate valve, turn off the valve, and turn the household water on again. Place a valve box around the gate valve. If the meter is in the basement or under the house, cut into the main line next to the meter and run the irrigation line out through the wall. In warm climates, you may find the household line exposed outside where it enters the house or at hose bibbs. You can cut into it at any spot, but the farther from the meter and the more connections the water must run through, the greater will be the pressure loss from friction.

Run Schedule 40 PVC to the manifold location or the location of the first valve, and stuff the end with a rag to keep dirt from entering while you work on the manifold.

The manifold consists of an antisiphon valve to prevent water from the garden from being siphoned into the household water, a valve for each sprinkler circuit, and pipe and fittings to connect them all. Assemble the manifold at a shop bench or convenient work spot.

If you are building a manual system, select valves that have a built-in antisiphon device. The most common types of antisiphon devices, called atmospheric vacuum breakers, must be installed at an elevation 6 inches higher than the highest sprinkler head in the system. This means that the atmospheric vacuum breaker is above the ground, sometimes a couple of feet above it. (If your site is steep, provide backflow protection with check valves, which don't require this height differential.) Check with your plumbing inspector or irrigation parts supplier for local requirements.

Valve Manifold

Valves

Line from water source

Lines to sprinkler heads

Electric valves are usually placed underground and accessed through valve boxes. It is frequently convenient to gang them in a manifold, but not necessary; they can be located anyplace. A pair of wires must run from the controller to each valve.

Attach the manifold to the line, turn off the valves, and open the gate valve to check joints for leakage. If nothing leaks, you can fill in the ditches to the manifold.

Lay out one circuit at a time. Beginning at the valve, cut and attach each fitting or pipe in its turn until you reach the sprinkler head. Attach the sprinkler head loosely for now, just to keep dirt out of the line.

Position lawn heads at the height you expect the final grade to be. Lawn heads next to sidewalks or edgings should be 3 inches from the edge, to allow room for lawn-edging equipment.

When all the lines are installed, remove the heads and turn on the circuits one at a time to flush any dirt out of the lines. As soon as each circuit is flushed, attach the heads again. Leaving the ditches open, stop for 24 hours to allow the solvent to set, so you can test the system.

Test the system by turning on one circuit at a time and adjusting the heads. If the water does not cover the area it was planned to cover, move heads or add heads to achieve complete coverage. When you are satisfied that all the circuits are working properly, backfill the ditches. As you backfill, leave a slight depression in the ditch, perhaps 2 inches deep. Remove the heads once more and turn on the system slightly to fill the ditches with water, settling the backfill. Replace the heads. After the backfill soil has drained enough, finish filling the ditches, leaving a slight mound over the ditch in lawn areas to accommodate later settling.

Drip Systems

Most of a drip system—the hose and emitters—is so simple to install and remove that it is treated as a temporary system; hose and emitters are added and removed as needs change. The hose can be put in either during or after planting; emitters are installed in the line after the planting is done.

Now, however, is the time to install any buried lines that carry water for a drip system to the back of the yard. If you wish, you can install permanent drip heads at this stage. Components for drip heads are available with

Draining the Line in Freezing Climates

In areas where the ground freezes to the depth of the irrigation lines, the lines must be drained each fall to prevent water in them from freezing and rupturing the pipe. This is most easily done with automatic drain valves, which drain the line automatically every time the water is shut off.

To enable the line to drain completely, slope the pipe toward each drain valve. Every low spot in the system of lines must be drained with an automatic drain valve, so the more carefully you plan the slope, the fewer valves you will need.

Wherever a drain valve is to be installed, to the side of the ditch dig an area about 1 foot square. It should be about 8 inches deeper than the ditch. Place a tee in the line and install the drain so it slopes down slightly from the pipe. Slip a short length of pipe over it to protect the opening. Add drain rock or gravel, filling the hole and covering the drain. Lay a sheet of plastic film across the gravel. Backfill the hole, covering the plastic with soil. The drain valve will drain the line into the pocket of gravel.

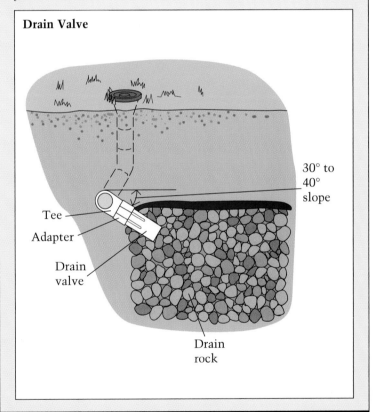

Drain Valve

30° to 40° slope

Tee

Adapter

Drain valve

Drain rock

either pipe thread, for permanent installation, or hose thread, for temporary installation.

Run lines as described in the section about installing hose bibbs (opposite page). Install a gate valve as a shutoff valve for the system. Then install a timer, a backflow prevention valve, a pressure reducer, and a filter. Attach the hose and emitters after planting, as described on page 89.

Completing Your Landscape

*You're almost done! Prepare the soil, install
the plants and finishing touches, and then enjoy
your low-cost landscape.*

If you've cleaned up after your last task, your yard looks neat and or-
derly. The paths, patios, and structures are in place, and the ground
is shaped about the way you want it. But it still looks barren. In this
chapter, you will learn how to prepare the soil and plant. When you
complete it, you will have a finished landscape.

The soil is the foundation of any planting. Any attention you give
to it before planting will pay you back with years of healthy plants. If it
is not in the best of shape now—if the topsoil has been stripped off
or is thin or drains poorly—you can improve it with a generous application of organic matter. If you have time, add organic matter more
than once, and allow it to decompose. As it rots in the soil, it creates
humus—a soft, dark substance that is one of the most important
differences between poor soil and good soil.

*Before planting, till large amounts of compost into the soil. If an area will be
closely planted, as a flower bed is, add organic material to the entire area. If
plants will be widely spaced, add compost around each plant.*

PREPARING THE SOIL FOR PLANTING

Vigorous, trouble-free plants depend on healthy soil. As far as a plant is concerned, healthy soil is soil that drains quickly but holds lots of water, is neither too acidic nor too alkaline, and contains the minerals the plant needs.

Where plants are spaced more than 2 feet apart, dig a hole for each plant and backfill with improved soil. Improved soil consists of the soil you dug out of the hole, with organic material and fertilizer mixed in. You can mix it in a wheelbarrow or in a pile on the ground.

Where plants are spaced less than 2 feet apart, prepare the soil over the whole area. Spread soil amendments before tilling, so the tilling incorporates them into the soil. Depending on your equipment, tilling usually mixes them into the top 6 to 8 inches of soil.

Considering Minerals and pH

Plants need 14 minerals for optimum health. Most soils have enough of all but three. One of these—nitrogen—is needed in all soils. Two others—potassium and phosphorus—are needed in parts of the country that get regular summer rainfall, but usually not in the arid West.

It's possible to test your soil for minerals, but it's usually easier and cheaper to fertilize when you plant and every spring after that. If you live in an arid climate, select a fertilizer high in nitrogen. If you live in a wet climate, select one that contains ample amounts of nitrogen, phosphorus, and potassium. Apply the quantities recommended on the fertilizer package.

You should, however, test your soil for acidity. In some states, the cooperative extension service will test your soil for a nominal fee. In states without this service find a soil laboratory (under "Laboratories" in the classified pages of the telephone book). You can also easily test your own soil with a kit from a garden center.

Soil acidity is measured in pH (which stands for potential H, or potential hydrogen), on a scale that ranges from 1 (the most acidic) to 14 (the most alkaline), with 7 being neutral. Most plants grow best in soil with a pH from 5.5 to 7.5. If your soil is more acidic than this, with a pH below 5.5, add limestone according to the table at left. If the pH is higher than 7.5, add sulfur according to the same table.

Incorporating Organic Matter

No matter what soil problems you start with, from heavy clay that drains too slowly to light sandy soil that dries up too quickly, the best thing you can do for your soil is to add lots of organic matter. For the soil, organic matter refers to plant material, either fresh or in some state of decomposition. Sawdust and straw are two of the most common soil additives. Compost, leaf mold, and manure are some of the best. You can also use peanut shells, pine needles, ground corncobs, or whatever is inexpensive in your area.

Organic matter opens up heavy clay by wedging the clay particles apart, allowing air and water to move freely through the soil. In sandy soil that dries too quickly (called droughty by farmers), the organic matter acts like a sponge, holding water and nutrients until the plant needs them.

After the initial landscaping, incorporate more organic matter whenever you till the soil. In vegetable beds and annual flower borders, this will be before every planting. For the rest of the garden, lightly spread compost or manure

---

Correcting pH

To make soil more alkaline, add ground limestone in the quantities shown in the table that follows. Wait a week and test the soil again. If necessary, add more limestone. Test the soil at least every other year. In southern and coastal states, reduce the application by approximately one half.

Ground Limestone: Amounts to Raise Soil pH
(pounds of ground limestone per 1,000 square feet)

Desired pH	Sand	Sandy Loam	Silt Loam	Clay Loam	Loam
4.0 to 6.5	60	115	161	193	230
4.5 to 6.5	51	96	133	161	193
5.0 to 6.5	41	78	106	129	152
5.5 to 6.5	28	60	78	92	106
6.0 to 6.5	14	32	41	51	55

To make the soil more acidic, add soil sulfur as shown in the table that follows. Sulfur is slower to change the pH of the soil than limestone, so wait a month before retesting.

Soil Sulfur: Amounts to Lower Soil pH
(pounds of soil sulfur per 1,000 square feet)

Desired pH	Sand	Loam	Clay
8.5 to 6.5	46	57	69
8.0 to 6.5	28	34	46
7.5 to 6.5	11	18	23
7.0 to 6.5	2	4	7

before you renew a mulch, or every year or so. Raindrops and earthworms will slowly work the additive into the soil for you.

Whenever possible, let natural organic matter decompose where it falls. If leaves are not suffocating a lawn or small plants, let them remain. Let grass clippings remain on the lawn to decompose.

If organic matter is dense, like manure or some types of sawdust, spread it 2 inches deep. If it is loose and fluffy, like straw, spread it 6 inches deep.

Tilling

Tilling mixes minerals and organic matter into the soil. It also loosens the soil to let air and water penetrate and makes a loose planting bed that is easy to dig in.

Rent a walk-behind rotary tiller for yards up to ¼ acre. For larger yards, rent a tractor with a rotary tiller attachment, or hire a contractor to till the yard for you. Rent the largest, heaviest tiller you can find. When breaking new ground, the heavier the tiller, the easier the work. Light tillers are made for stirring the soil in established vegetable gardens and flower beds; they bounce over the top of new ground without digging in properly.

Heavy clay soil is easiest to work with when it contains just the right amount of moisture. Too dry, it is hard and rocklike; too wet, it is plastic and sticky. When just right, the soil can be turned over with a shovel, and the clods break apart when struck. If the soil is too dry, water it thoroughly and wait about 3 days for it to dry to the right consistency. Moisture has less effect on sandy soils, which can be worked when they are wet or dry.

INSTALLING HEADERS

Headers divide plantings in the garden. The most useful headers are those around a lawn, where they simplify trimming. Headers also confine mulch; make neat, sharp divisions between plantings; and give a tidy, professional look to a landscape.

A mowing strip is a ground-level header wide enough to run a lawnmower wheel on, allowing the mower blades to mow right to the edge of the lawn. It is usually of concrete or brick set in concrete, 4 to 8 inches wide.

Begin concrete headers or mowing strips by excavating a trench 8 inches deep and 4 to 8

inches wide for a mowing strip, 2 inches wide for a header. Tamp 4 inches of base rock into the trench, then build forms 4 inches high. Straight forms can be made of 2 by 4s. Create curves from benderboard or ¼-inch plywood or hardboard strips. Pour concrete in the forms and finish as described on pages 68 to 70.

Make brick headers by setting brick in concrete as described on page 66, in the section on making edges for dry-laid brick. Bricks can also be placed upright in a trench at least 6 inches deep and just wide enough to hold the brick. Cut the edges of the trench with a spade, using a board as a straightedge, then dig out the soil between the cuts with a mattock. If the area is already tilled, set the bricks, then tamp the soil on each side of them to hold them in place.

Make straight wooden headers of 2 by 4s set on edge. Use foundation-grade redwood or pressure-treated lumber. Dig trenches a couple of inches wider than the header, using a mattock. Set the 2 by 4s in place, anchoring them with stakes every 4 feet and at board ends. Drive the stakes about an inch lower than the header top, or saw off the tops of the stakes at a 45-degree angle. Fill the trench, covering the stake heads.

You can make curved headers with triple thicknesses of benderboard or with 1-inch lumber cut with saw kerfs. Dig trenches a couple of inches wider than the board. Wet one board, place it in the trench, and pound in temporary stakes to hold the board in place. Once the

A mowing strip is a narrow concrete path dividing the lawn from the flower bed. One wheel of the lawnmower rides on the strip, making edging a lawn a quicker task.

board is correctly positioned, drive in permanent stakes every 3 feet, at every joint, and on either side of the board at the ends. Drive the stakes an inch lower than the top of the board.

If you are using benderboard, nail one board to each stake by placing the head of a sledgehammer behind the stake and nailing against it. Nail a second board against the face of each staked board. Then add a third board, all with the joints staggered. Place stakes at each joint. After all boards are nailed to stakes, pin the tops of the layers together with 6-penny (6d) box nails every 6 inches. Drive the nails at a 45-degree angle against a sledgehammer head.

The nail will turn when it strikes the hammer and clinch into the back of the benderboard, holding the boards tightly together.

Heavy, rustic headers can also be made of railroad ties or 4 by 4 lumber. Pin these to the ground by drilling holes and driving concrete reinforcing rods (rebar) through them and into the ground a foot or so. Sink the head of the rebar in the tie or cut it off flush.

Metal headers can be purchased in ⅛-inch iron or anodized aluminum, in 16-foot strips. They come with steel pins to hold them to the ground. Garden centers can also supply corrugated aluminum edging material, which will

---

Bending Lumber With Saw Kerfs

¼" of uncut wood

Position of kerfs in a tight bend, viewed from above

With a table saw set to cut through all but ¼" of a ¾" board, cut saw kerfs in the area to be bent. For tighter bends, make the kerfs closer together

---

Nailing Benderboards Together

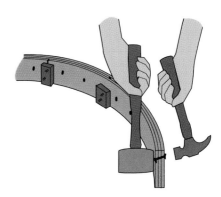

Nail the tops of benderboards together by clinching every 6" with a 6d nail driven at an angle against a hammer head

---

Raised Beds

Planting beds can be raised above ground level to make them easier to reach and work in, or just to add another dimension to an otherwise flat garden. Since the soil they will hold is heavy, the beds should be of substantial material. Wooden beds, like any wood in contact with the soil, should be made of redwood or cedar heartwood, or pressure-treated lumber.

The structure that forms a raised bed can also be made of broken sidewalk built to form four retaining walls. See page 62 for instructions.

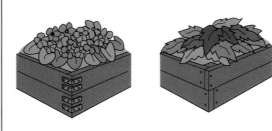

Soil exerts significant pressure on the sides of the beds. Use lumber at least 2" thick, fastening the corners with angle irons or nailing them to a stout stake

not last very long in the landscape, and several plastic edging materials.

After installing headers, rake the soil to its final contours, using the headers to establish the grade. If the soil is still fluffy from tilling, leave it about an inch higher than the headers and walks; it will settle with the first rain.

PLANTING TREES AND SHRUBS

If you have trees and shrubs in containers that are gallon-sized or larger, follow the planting directions in this section. If you have smaller plants or are planting seedlings or rooted cuttings, follow the directions on page 87.

Try to plant just before the season most favorable to the plants. In many areas, this is early spring. In mild-winter regions, fall is also a good time. However, planting can be done at any time of the year the soil can be worked—the plants will just need more attention. If the soil is dry, water it thoroughly and let it drain for a few days before planting.

Planting From Containers

Following your plan, place each tree and shrub, in its container, in its intended location. Study the effect, then make any adjustments in placement. Once you have all the locations just right, dig a hole where each plant is sitting, making the hole a little shallower than the height of the rootball and about twice as wide. Mix the soil from the hole with fertilizer, lime or sulfur, and organic matter as described on page 82. The organic matter should make up about one quarter of the total mix.

To remove plants from cans, invert them and tap the rim on a hard surface to loosen the soil. You will now be able to pull out the plant without disturbing the rootball too much. Make three vertical cuts about an inch deep around the outside of the rootball. This cuts through any roots that are circling the can and stimulates new growth at the cut.

Many trees are sold in 15-gallon cans. Before planting, use a hatchet to remove the bottom of the can. Using the handles on the can, lower the tree into the hole. Once it is in position, cut the can away from the rootball.

After the plants are in their holes, cover the rootball with the improved soil. Do not cover any part of the trunk or main stem; in some plants it causes a fatal disease called crown rot. As you backfill, build a low berm around the rootball to make a watering basin.

Fill the basin with water. Before the hole drains, while the backfill soil is still soupy, shake the plant gently to remove any air pockets in the soil. You can also adjust its height and turn its best face toward the front.

Planting Field-Grown Plants

Field-grown plants will not be in containers. Either the rootball will be wrapped in burlap, or the roots will be bare.

Field-grown evergreens are dug during the planting season and sold with a ball of soil around their roots. For protection, the ball is

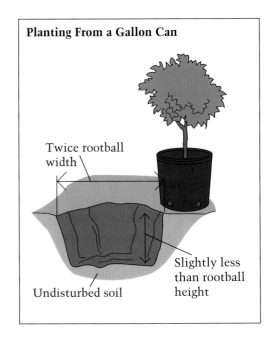

Planting From a Gallon Can

Twice rootball width

Slightly less than rootball height

Undisturbed soil

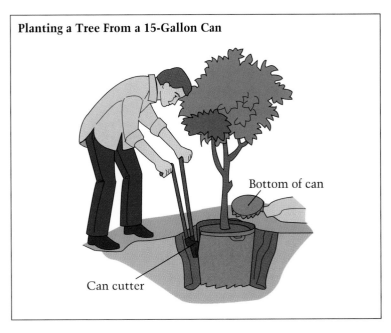

Planting a Tree From a 15-Gallon Can

Bottom of can

Can cutter

wrapped in burlap and tied with twine. To plant a field-grown evergreen, dig a hole and prepare the soil as if you were planting a containerized plant (see the previous section). Set the rootball in the hole, with the burlap still in place. If the fabric or the twine that ties it is made of plastic, cut most of it away. If it is jute, remove the twine and fold the burlap into the hole. Complete the planting process, following the instructions for planting containerized plants.

Field-grown deciduous trees and shrubs are usually dug in late winter, without any soil around their roots. To plant a bare-root tree, prepare the soil and dig a hole large enough to accommodate the roots without cramping them. Place the tree so the top root will be an inch below soil level. Hold the tree in position as you fill in the hole, working the soil around the roots. Make a watering basin around the tree and water it thoroughly. While the soil is still soupy, shake the tree to remove air pockets in the soil, then settle the soil around the roots.

Staking Trees

Stakes are temporary supports for trees that need them (bare-root trees seldom need staking). If the tree will stay upright, don't stake it at all. If it leans under its own weight or threatens to topple out of its hole in the wind, put in a stake—not the flimsy training stake that came with the tree, but a strong one, at least $1\frac{1}{2}$ inches in diameter.

Position the stake on the upwind side of the tree. Drive it into the ground just outside the edge of the rootball, deep enough that it is secure in the undisturbed soil at the bottom of the hole.

Tie the tree loosely to the stake with a rubber tie, soft rope, or a piece of wire inside a length of garden hose. The tie should be as low as it can be and still support the tree. The tree should be free to move in the wind; this movement will strengthen it so it will eventually outgrow the need for staking. Cut off the stake just above the tie. In very windy locations, drive a stake on each side of the tree and tie the tree to each stake.

Installing Hedges

Hedge shrubs are usually purchased in gallon-sized cans. Plant them like other plants in gallon cans, placing them 18 to 30 inches apart. (Most plants will fill in at the wider spacing, but

the resulting hedge will take an extra year or so to look finished.) If plants are purchased with bare roots, plant them in a trench and space them as you would space plants in gallon cans.

To establish a strong root system, let the plants grow for a year without pruning. Then, in early spring, cut them off 6 inches above the ground. After that, every time the plants grow 4 inches, shear them lightly, removing $\frac{1}{2}$ inch of new growth from both the top and sides. Frequent shearing forces shrubs to grow thick. Sheared shrubs make a more attractive hedge sooner than unsheared shrubs.

Once the hedge has reached a minimum adequate height, slow its growth by shearing almost all the new growth off at every pruning, allowing only $\frac{1}{4}$ inch of new growth to remain. The hedge will remain green and dense when it is allowed some growth.

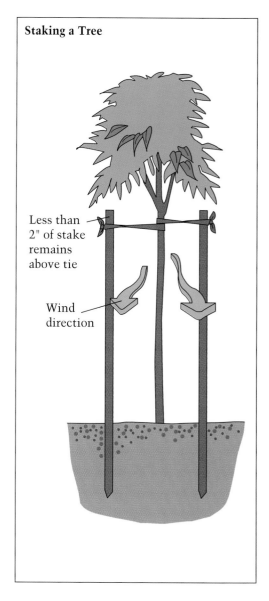

Staking a Tree

Less than 2" of stake remains above tie

Wind direction

To create a formal hedge, prune it so it has a flat top, flat sides, and sharp corners. You will need to shear it several times a year to maintain the crisp look. To create an informal hedge, shear it into a rounded, natural shape. After it has reached the minimum acceptable height, prune it yearly to slow growth and keep the plants dense. To keep the hedge dense right to the ground, slant the sides slightly, so it is wider at the bottom than the top. This allows light to reach the bottom branches.

PERENNIALS, GROUND COVERS, AND BEDDING PLANTS

Perennials and ground covers in gallon cans are planted in the same way trees and shrubs in gallon cans are. Planting techniques for smaller plants depend on the type of container in which they are planted.

Where plants will be close together, the easiest course is to till the entire planting bed. Before planting, amend and till the planting bed as described on pages 82 and 83.

Planting From Small Containers

Set out plants in plastic containers in the planting bed. Study the effect and adjust their positions as needed. Space the plants evenly over the entire planting area. If the plants are expected to fill in the area, as ground covers are, set them out on a diagonal grid, as shown in the illustration below.

If plants are in six-packs, space the packs at regular intervals over the planting bed. Remove the plants from one pack at a time, pushing the rootball up from the bottom to loosen it, then shaking the plant gently out into your hand.

Holes for smaller plants can be dug most easily with a trowel. Stab the trowel into the soil and pull it toward you, bringing out a trowelful of soil. Drop the plant into the hole. In one motion scoop the soil around the plant and pat it down with your hands.

Some biodegradable containers, such as peat pots, can be planted with the plant. Tear the rims off peat pots above the soil line. This will prevent them from wicking water from the soil and drying the rootball. Heavy fiberboard containers used for larger plants are also biodegradable, but they degrade slowly. Either cut the pot off the rootball or slash the sides and bottom in several places to keep the container from restricting root growth. Remove the rims from these pots, also.

Planting From Flats

Although plants in flats may look as if the entire flat is covered with plants, they are actually planted in neat rows. A week before planting,

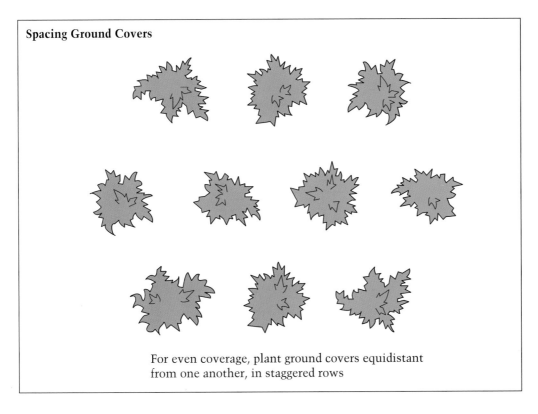

Spacing Ground Covers

For even coverage, plant ground covers equidistant from one another, in staggered rows

cut between these rows in both directions, to separate the plants into individual blocks. During the week before planting, the cut roots will begin to regrow within the soil block. The resulting root system will be denser than if you cut or tore them apart at planting time.

Remove plants from the flat and plant them, one at a time, with a trowel. Press each firmly into the soil and smooth the soil between plants as you work.

Water the bed thoroughly as soon as you finish planting. If the weather is hot, keep it moist for the next couple of weeks. If the weather is very hot and dry, shade the plants lightly. An easy way to shade them is to scatter straw across the planting, using just enough to protect the plants from the hot sun without depriving them of light.

In nature, soil is seldom exposed to sun and air. Instead, it is covered with leaves, dead grass, and fallen twigs. Besides providing nutrients to the soil as it rots, the organic material on the surface slows evaporation and insulates the soil, preventing it from becoming too hot or cold. Imitate nature and insulate the roots of your plants by adding a mulch in a 2- or 3-inch layer all around the plants.

A permanent mulch may be made of rock, gravel, or bark chunks, which will not rot or degrade. However, on clay soil, if walked on when wet, they will disappear into the soil.

More transient mulches can be made of the same organic materials you added to the soil to improve it. Leaves, needles, and leaf mold add a natural look. These organic mulches need annual replenishing, but they improve the soil as they decompose.

Planting Seeds

Although landscapers seldom seed anything except lawns, working from seed is the least expensive way to plant. Many seeds need specific conditions to germinate. Refer to one of the books recommended on page 92 for instructions. Most seeds are started in indoor flats and raised in containers until the plants are a few inches high and ready to be planted outside.

Seeds of plants native to your area will germinate if you imitate nature. To plant a native oak, for instance, gather acorns when they fall and plant them a couple of inches deep where you want an oak tree. To be sure of getting a tree in that location, plant three acorns and remove the two weakest plants after germination.

To carpet an area with plants such as ground covers or wildflowers, follow the directions for planting lawns from seed, which appear later in this chapter.

The shredded bark used as a mulch in this new landscape is attractive and will last for several years. As it weathers, it will flatten and turn a soft gray that sets off plant colors nicely.

PUTTING IN A DRIP SYSTEM

A drip system begins at the drip head, a collection of valves and fittings that controls, measures, or conditions the water for the system. The drip head can be screwed onto a hose bibb or cut into a water line at any convenient place. Starting at the connection, the drip head includes these parts, in approximately this order:

Shutoff valve   If you are connecting to a hose bibb, the bibb is the shutoff. Otherwise, you will install a gate valve to shut off the system.

Timer   Simple electric or battery-operated timers are usually used with drip systems.

Backflow prevention valve   This device prevents water from the drip system (which might contain toxic chemicals or bacterial contaminants) from being drawn into your household water supply.

Pressure reducer   This valve lowers the pressure from household pressure to 15 to 30 pounds per square inch.

Filter   Because the small openings in a drip system clog easily, any particles must be removed from the water. If you have clean city water, a simple filter will serve. If you have well water or other unfiltered water, you'll need a sophisticated filter.

Other head components, available but not necessary, include a fertilizer injector which feeds small amounts of fertilizer into the water, and meters that let you monitor flow rate or water pressure. The rest of the system consists of hose and emitters.

Hose   Because of the low pressure, water is carried in flexible polyethylene tubing called hose. It can be cut with a knife, and the fittings are simple push-on types that don't need clamps or glue.

Emitters   These components control the drip of water. Most are preset to emit from ½ to 5 gallons per hour. They punch into the hose anyplace they are needed. One emitter will wet a piece of ground about a foot in diameter, enough for one small plant. Larger plants need more emitters. A rosebush, for example, needs three to five emitters; large trees need many more than that.

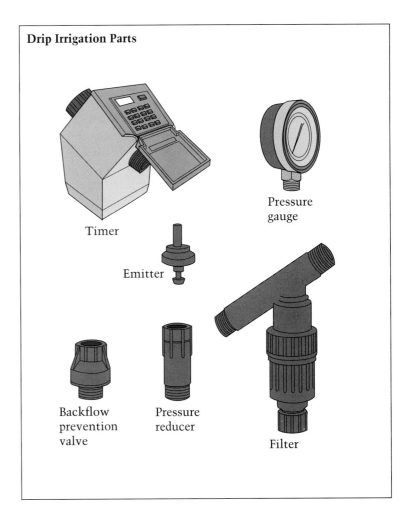

Drip Irrigation Parts

Timer

Pressure gauge

Emitter

Backflow prevention valve

Pressure reducer

Filter

Placing the Hose

Select a hose pattern that will take hose to each of the plants it must water. Attach the hose to the drip head and lay it out through the entire garden, splitting it with tees wherever necessary. Run the hose over the rootball of every plant. Because the pressure needed is so low, one circuit is enough for all but very large yards; you will be able to water the entire yard with a single setting. Cap the ends with removable caps to allow periodic flushing.

Punch a hole with a special punch or a 16d nail wherever you want an emitter, and push the barbed emitter into the hole. That's all there is to it. Place one emitter over the rootball of each small plant for now. Plants that were in 5-gallon cans or larger containers will need either a second emitter or an emitter that drips faster.

The hose can be left exposed, but it isn't very attractive. Cover it with mulch, or use a hoe to scrape a shallow trench, drop the hose in, and cover it with soil. (Remember that you need access to the hose to check and repair it and to add emitters. Don't get carried away with trenching.) Before you dig in the garden, locate the drip hose so you can avoid piercing it with a shovel.

Fine-tuning the System

Set the timer so the system is on for about an hour each day. At first, set it for the time of day when you are most likely to be in the garden, so you can see how the system is working. Check the soil under a few emitters shortly before the system is due to turn on. If the soil isn't damp enough to feel cool and to wet your finger slightly, increase the length of time the system is on. If the soil makes your finger muddy, decrease the time. As the plants grow, increase the length of time the system is on. The soil should be wet under each drip emitter and a few inches to each side. Roots will proliferate in this wet area, adapting the plant to the system. Depending on the flow rate of the emitters, your garden soil, and the weather, the system may need to be on from one hour to many hours per day.

To give more water to an individual plant, add more emitters over its roots. A tree or large shrub needs more emitters as it grows larger. Emitters can be removed by pulling them from the line and replacing them with "goof plugs."

Monitor the system carefully. Lines can pull loose, and the tiny orifices in emitters plug up easily. Especially in hot weather, be alert for any plant that looks as if it isn't getting enough water. Increase the length of watering time as the days lengthen in spring and decrease it again with shortening fall days. The hose and emitters won't be harmed by freezing, but drain or remove the drip head if you live in an area where winter could mean frozen plumbing.

PUTTING IN LAWNS

Because the installation of a sod lawn can be done so quickly, sod lawns are becoming the standard of landscapers. However, lawns planted from seed, sprigs, or plugs are just as satisfactory as sod lawns, and they are much less expensive. This section presents directions for creating these inexpensive lawns. If you wish to put in a sod lawn, the sod dealer will give you full instructions.

The best time to plant a lawn is just before the weather changes to that most favorable to the type of grass you are planting. Grasses adapted to northern climates—bluegrass, bentgrass, ryegrass, and fescue—grow best in cool weather. In mild-climate areas, plant them in the fall; where winters are severe, plant in early spring. Grasses adapted to southern climates grow best in hot weather. Plant them in mid- or late spring, just before hot weather.

Level the lawn area thoroughly. Any settling causes dips and humps, which are hard to mow and water properly, and leveling the surface is difficult after the lawn is established. Water the soil to settle it, allow it to drain, then roll it with a rented roller. (Some nurseries will loan you a roller when you buy grass seed.) If the soil is clay, and drains poorly, don't use a roller—rolling will exacerbate drainage problems. If the settling or rolling create any high or low spots, level them with a rake, then water and roll again. Repeat until the ground remains level after rolling. As you are leveling, rake off any lumps to make a smooth, fine seedbed.

To get the new lawn off to a fast start, spread 15 pounds of a balanced fertilizer (about 15 percent each of nitrogen, phosphorus, and potassium) per 1,000 square feet of lawn. Water the area to dissolve and dilute the fertilizer, and let the soil drain.

Planting Seed

A cooperative extension adviser, the nursery worker, or the grass seed label will tell you how much seed to sow. With a rented or borrowed spreader, spread the lawn seed evenly. Next, drag a lawn rake behind you over the lawn. Don't use a raking motion as if you were raking leaves; just let the tines stir the seed into the top ¼ inch of soil.

With a light lawn roller half-filled with water, roll the lawn to press the seed into the soil. Spread a light mulch of straw or sawdust—enough to barely cover the soil without excluding light. This helps keep the surface moist. Now water the lawn by hand, using the gentlest spray possible to avoid dislodging the seeds. Keep the surface moist until the seeds germinate. In hot, dry weather, you may need to water more than once a day. If available, composted sawdust is a user-friendly mulch because it changes color dramatically as it dries out, making it easy to see when you need to water again.

Some grass seeds germinate in a week, but most take up to four weeks. When the grass is about 2 inches high, feed it again. Use 5 pounds of fertilizer per 1,000 square feet. Water it in well. Repeat this light feeding every month for the first growing season.

Mow the lawn for the first time when the grass is about 3 inches tall. Use a sharp reel mower, if one is available, to keep from pulling out the tiny plants.

Planting Sprigs

If the soil is dry, water it a day before planting. With a hoe, dig furrows 2 inches deep and 6 inches apart. Since sprigs dry out and die very quickly, keep them cool and moist until you are ready to plant them. Depending on the weather, work in sections that you can plant in just a few minutes, so the sprigs don't dry out. Plant only a few at a time, cover them with soil, and water them before continuing.

Lay the sprigs 6 inches apart in the furrows, with the green blades above soil level and the white stems below. After laying out one section, pull soil over the furrow with a rake, leaving the green blades exposed. Smooth the surface and water the planted area.

After the entire lawn is planted, roll it with a half-filled roller to firm the soil around the sprigs. Keep the soil moist for a couple of weeks, until the sprigs are established.

Planting Plugs

Plugs are sections of sod about 3 inches across. Plant them 6 to 12 inches apart. Dig holes with a trowel or a plugger—a tool that punches holes just the right size for the plug. Place a plug in a hole and firm the soil around it. Roll the lawn with a light roller (half-filled) to settle the plugs and level the grade. If the soil between plugs settles, leaving a bumpy surface, spread soil to level the lawn again.

Plugs are less susceptible than seeds or sprigs to drying, but it is still important to keep the soil damp for the first couple of weeks.

GARDEN ORNAMENTS AND FURNITURE

Garden ornaments and furniture can have a dramatic impact on the appearance and ambience of a garden. They contribute powerfully to the sense of style and can even modify an existing style. A set of ornate white wrought-iron chairs and tables adds a Victorian or old-fashioned feel to a garden setting. Wooden

Adirondack chairs are always casual, and carved teak benches add elegance.

Garden ornaments can consist of traditional sundials, glass balls, and birdbaths, or less traditional items such as antique farm tools, modern art, and found objects. Traditionally, furnishing the garden can involve more stylistic freedom than decorating the house. Gardens lend themselves to whimsy and might include droll assemblages or folk art that express the humor, interests, or personality of the gardener.

Once the furniture is in place, your landscape is ready to be enjoyed. Do any final cleaning up—those "temporary" piles of bricks have a habit of taking up residence—pour yourself a tall iced tea, and enjoy your garden.

A touch of whimsy is not out of place in a garden. These manhole covers came from a wrecking yard.

Sources

Mail-Order Pond Supplies

Lilypons Water Gardens
Box 10
Buckeystown, MD 21717-0010
Plants, fish, books, and equipment

Paradise Water Gardens
62 May Street
Whitman, MA 02382
Plants, books, and equipment

Slocum Water Gardens
1101 Cypress Gardens Boulevard
Winter Haven, FL 33884
Plants, books, fish, and equipment

Van Ness Water Gardens
2460 North Euclid Avenue
Upland, CA 91768-1199
Plants, fish, books, and equipment

Waterford Gardens
74 East Allendale Road
Saddle River, NJ 07458
Plants, fish, books, and equipment

Irrigation Supplies

The Urban Farmer Store
2833 Vicente Street
San Francisco, CA 94116
*Irrigation supplies, including drip
irrigation materials*

Plants and Seeds

Applewood Seed Co.
Box 10761, Edgemont Station
Golden, CO 80401
Wildflower seeds

Edible Landscaping
Box 77
Afton, VA 22920
Attractive fruit tree and berry plants

J. L. Hudson, Seedsman
Box 1058
Redwood City, CA 94064
Wide variety of seeds

Lawyer Nursery
950 Highway 200 West
Plains, MT 59859
Seeds and liners for trees and shrubs

Plants of the Southwest
Route 6, Box 11A
Santa Fe, NM 87501
Southwest tree, shrub, and flower seeds

F. W. Schumacher Co.
Sandwich, MA 02563
Tree and shrub seeds

Sheffield's Seed Co.
273 Route 34
Locke, NY 13092
Tree and shrub seeds

Recommended Books

Building Stone Walls, by John
Vivian. Garden Way. 1985.
*Complete instructions for making
walls out of field stone.*

***The Complete Book of Edible
Landscaping,*** by Rosalind Creasy.
Sierra Club Books, San Francisco.
1982.

***Designing and Maintaining Your
Edible Landscape Naturally,*** by
Robert Kourik. Metamorphic Press,
Box 1841, Santa Rosa, CA 95402. 1986.
*Both of the above are excellent books.
Creasy's focuses on the subject of
edible landscaping. Kourik's fertile
mind is less restrained; his book
offers a wealth of information on all
aspects of landscaping.*

Deck Plans, by Robert J. Beckstrom.
Ortho Books. 1985.
*Ten plans for different kinds of decks,
each with instructions for modifying
to fit your house and lot.*

***Environmentally Friendly
Gardening: Easy Composting,***
by Jeff Ball and Robert Kourick.
Ortho Books. 1992.
Complete composting instructions.

Garden Pools & Fountains, by
Edward B. Claflin and Charles B.
Thomas. Ortho Books. 1988.
*Basic instructions for making and
caring for lily ponds and fish ponds.*

***How to Design & Build Decks &
Patios***, by Lin Cotton and T. Jeff
Williams. Ortho Books. 1979.
*Basic instructions for building decks,
including attachment to houses, hill-
side problems, etc.*

***How to Design & Build Fences &
Gates,*** by Diane Snow. Ortho Books.
1985.
*Instructions and plans for many
different styles of fences and gates.*

***Plant Propagation for the Amateur
Gardener,*** by John I. Wright. U.S.
distributor: Sterling Publishing, New
York. 1983.
*Well illustrated and detailed without
being too technical. Includes discus-
sions of starting seeds and rooting
cuttings.*

***The Reference Manual of Woody
Plant Propagation,*** by Michael A.
Dirr and Charles W. Heuser, Jr. Varsity
Press, Box 6301, Athens, GA 30604.
1987.
*A bit technical, but it has all you
need to know to germinate any woody
seed or root any cutting.*

U.S. Measure and Metric Measure Conversion Chart

Formulas for Exact Measures					Rounded Measures for Quick Reference		
	Symbol	When you know:	Multiply by:	To find:			
Mass (weight)	oz	ounces	28.35	grams	1 oz		= 30 g
	lb	pounds	0.45	kilograms	4 oz		= 115 g
	g	grams	0.035	ounces	8 oz		= 225 g
	kg	kilograms	2.2	pounds	16 oz	= 1 lb	= 450 g
					32 oz	= 2 lb	= 900 g
					36 oz	= 2¼ lb	= 1000 g (1 kg)
Volume	pt	pints	0.47	liters	1 c	= 8 oz	= 250 ml
	qt	quarts	0.95	liters	2 c (1 pt)	= 16 oz	= 500 ml
	gal	gallons	3.785	liters	4 c (1 qt)	= 32 oz	= 1 liter
	ml	milliliters	0.034	fluid ounces	4 qt (1 gal)	= 128 oz	= 3¾ liter
Length	in.	inches	2.54	centimeters	⅜ in.	= 1.0 cm	
	ft	feet	30.48	centimeters	1 in.	= 2.5 cm	
	yd	yards	0.9144	meters	2 in.	= 5.0 cm	
	mi	miles	1.609	kilometers	2½ in.	= 6.5 cm	
	km	kilometers	0.621	miles	12 in. (1 ft)	= 30 cm	
	m	meters	1.094	yards	1 yd	= 90 cm	
	cm	centimeters	0.39	inches	100 ft	= 30 m	
					1 mi	= 1.6 km	
Temperature	°F	Fahrenheit	$\frac{5}{9}$ (after subtracting 32)	Celsius	32° F	= 0° C	
	°C	Celsius	$\frac{9}{5}$ (then add 32)	Fahrenheit	212° F	= 100° C	
Area	in.^{2}	square inches	6.452	square centimeters	1 in.^{2}	= 6.5 cm^2	
	ft^2	square feet	929.0	square centimeters	1 ft^2	= 930 cm^2	
	yd^2	square yards	8361.0	square centimeters	1 yd^2	= 8360 cm^2	
	a.	acres	0.4047	hectares	1 a.	= 4050 m^2	